Soccer Practice Games

Joseph A. Luxbacher, PhD
Head Soccer Coach, University of Pittsburgh

Human Kinetics

Library of Congress Cataloging-in-Publication Data

Luxbacher, Joe.
    Soccer practice games / Joseph A. Luxbacher.
      p.   cm.
    ISBN 0-87322-554-6
    1. Soccer--Training. 2. Soccer--Coaching. I. Title.
    GV943.9.T7L895   1995
    796.334'07--dc20   94-12525
                                           CIP

ISBN: 0-87322-554-6

Developmental Editor: Anne Mischakoff Heiles; **Assistant Editors:** Jacqueline Blakley, Anna Curry, Ed Giles, John Wentworth, and Jennifer Wilson; **Copyeditor:** Kenneth Walker; **Proofreader:** Sue Fetters; **Typesetter & Page Layout:** Julie Overholt; **Text Designer:** Judy Henderson; **Cover Designer:** Jack Davis; **Cover Photographer:** Scott Barrow; **Illustrator:** Tim Offenstein; **Interior Photos:** Courtesy of Champaign Park District, Champaign, IL; **Printer:** United Graphics

Human Kinetics books are available at special discounts for bulk purchase. Special editions or book excerpts can also be created to specification. For details, contact the Special Sales Manager at Human Kinetics.

Printed in the United States of America   10   9

Human Kinetics
Web site: www.humankinetics.com

United States: Human Kinetics, P.O. Box 5076, Champaign, IL 61825-5076
800-747-4457
e-mail: humank@hkusa.com

Canada: Human Kinetics, 475 Devonshire Road, Unit 100, Windsor, ON N8Y 2L5
800-465-7301 (in Canada only)
e-mail: orders@hkcanada.com

Europe: Human Kinetics, Units C2/C3 Wira Business Park, West Park Ring Road
Leeds LS16 6EB, United Kingdom
+44 (0) 113 278 1708
e-mail: hk@hkeurope.com

Australia: Human Kinetics, 57A Price Avenue, Lower Mitcham, South Australia 5062
08 8277 1555
e-mail: liahka@senet.com.au

New Zealand: Human Kinetics, P.O. Box 105-231, Auckland Central
09-523-3462
e-mail: hkp@ihug.co.nz

To my late father, Francis Luxbacher, my first and finest coach. He conveyed a sincere love of the game to everyone who knew him. His presence is always with me.

Contents

Preface

Soccer, the world's most popular sport and the national game of nearly every country in Europe, South America, Asia, and Africa, has arrived and is taking America by storm. Known internationally as "football," the game provides a common language for peoples of diverse backgrounds and heritages, a bond that transcends political, ethnic, and religious barriers. Once considered by Americans to be a foreign sport, soccer is played today by more than 20 million Americans—girls, boys, women, and men. Among team sports it is second only to basketball in number of participants, and this number continues to grow each year.

A landmark event occurred in the summer of 1994 when, for the first time, the United States hosted soccer's international championship—the World Cup. The World Cup is generally regarded as the premier sporting event on the planet. Held every 4 years, the matches attract a following that dwarfs both our Super Bowl and our World Series. The emotion and excitement that surround the event are unparalleled in the realm of competitive athletics.

Soccer's universal appeal does not rest on it being an easy game to play. In fact, soccer may demand more of athletes than any other sport. Players must perform a variety of skills under the match pressures of restricted space, limited time, physical fatigue, and determined opponents. Knowledge of tactics and strategies is essential. Decision-making skills are constantly tested as players must respond instantly to myriad changing situations during play. With the exception of the goalkeeper there are no specialists on the soccer field. As in basketball and hockey, each player must be able to defend as well as attack. And although soccer players don't have to be of any particular size or shape, all must possess a high level of fitness. Field players may be required to run several miles during the course of a match. The physical and mental challenges confronting players are great. Individual and team performance ultimately depends on each player's ability to meet these challenges. Such ability requires development.

Soccer Practice Games has been written to provide players and coaches with a variety of games that will nurture the technical, tactical, and physical development of players. All exercises are designed to challenge players, to keep them active, interested, and involved. The games are competitive, fun to play, and can be easily adapted to a wide range of ages and abilities. Novice and experienced players alike respond more favorably if they are excited and enthused about what they are doing. The games described here are designed to create such an attitude. This does not imply that standard drills have no place in the training regimen. The optimal learning environment should include a balance between typical soccer drills and the games described in this book.

Acknowledgments

The writing and publishing of a book truly require a team effort. In that regard I am greatly indebted to a number of people for their help and cooperation with this project. Although it is not possible to mention everyone by name, I would like to express my deepest appreciation to the following individuals: the staff at Human Kinetics, particularly Ted Miller and Anne Mischakoff Heiles, for their insight, patience, and support in the development of the book; the staff coaches of Keystone Soccer Kamps and Shoot to Score Soccer Camps for their willingness to share ideas; my mother, Mary Ann Luxbacher, for her constant love and support of everything that I do; and most importantly my wife Gail, the love of my life, for her willingness to sacrifice personal time for writing time when the deadlines drew near. Her love, understanding, and support made the journey much more enjoyable.

How to Use This Book

Planning a practice that motivates kids to play, to learn, and to enjoy the game is one of the most important responsibilities of the soccer coach. Kids want and need to be excited, enthused, and entertained while they learn. They do not respond well to long-winded lectures, standing in line, or anything else that spells boredom. Young soccer players derive the most benefit from practices that are challenging and fun, from exercises that are activity oriented, from games in which they are constantly moving, touching the ball, and scoring goals. *Soccer Practice Games* was written with that fact in mind.

The book contains 120 gamelike activities and competitions that coaches can use to create an exciting and enjoyable learning environment. The games place players in controlled, competitive situations. They teach fundamentals and emphasize the skills and tactics necessary to become a complete player. The games are particularly useful for beginning and intermediate players, and they can also be an alternative to traditional training with older, more experienced players.

The book is organized into four parts: "Games for Warm-Up and Conditioning," "Games for Skill Training," "Games for Tactical Training," and "Games for Goalkeeper Training." In reality, most games emphasize two or more essential elements of the sport. For example, all of the games for tactical training involve a ball and require players to move continuously throughout the exercises. As a result players benefit from fitness and skill development in addition to the tactical knowledge derived from these games.

Games in the parts "Games for Skill Training" and "Games for Tactical Training" have been arranged in order of increasing complexity. The ordering is provided to assist coaches in choosing games that are most appropriate for their players. Expose novice players to the most basic games first and gradually progress to more mentally and physically challenging ones.

Most games are extremely versatile and can be easily adapted to the age and the ability of players. For example, coaches can make a game more challenging by

- placing restrictions on players (for example, require one- or two-touch passing only);
- adjusting the available space and time which players have to execute skills or tactics (the less space and time available the more difficult the challenge);
- increasing fitness demands by requiring more running and player movement;
- incorporating decision making into the exercise (for instance, require players to choose from one of several options when passing or receiving the ball); and
- adding the pressure of opponents—the ultimate challenge.

Best of all, whether the game is shaped to test the novice or challenge the experienced player, it remains fun and functional for everyone involved. Each game is organized in the following easily understood format:

- *Title.* In most cases, but not all, the title provides a general idea of what the game involves and emphasizes. For example, "Pass and Receive to Score" requires players to complete passes to teammates in order to score points. Some titles are not as obvious, however, and the coach should look to other headings (such as objectives) for more information on the game's utility.

- *Minutes.* A time frame is listed for each game. The minimum and maximum values are provided only as general guidelines, and should be adjusted to the age, ability, and physical limitations of players. The actual duration of a game should be the coach's decision since he or she probably knows the players better than anyone else.

- *Players.* Some games require a specific number of players, others do not. For example, "Playing the Wall" requires groups of 3 players since the game focuses entirely on the 2 vs. 1 situation. Other games, such as "Chain Tag" or "Passing by the Numbers," can involve a range of players. When determining how many players to include in a game always keep in mind that all players should be active and touching the ball most of the time. If too many players are involved, or too few balls, the game will not accomplish its objectives.

- *Objectives.* Most games have a primary objective and two or more closely associated secondary objectives. For example, the primary objective of the game "All vs. All" is to develop dribbling skills. Secondary objectives are the development of shielding and tackling skills and improved fitness. Using games that accomplish more than one objective is a form of economical training that makes the best use of limited practice time.

Coaches should also consider a game's objectives to determine whether it fits into the general theme of a specific training session. For example, if the primary focus of a practice is the development of passing and receiving skills, the games selected for the session should fit that criterion.

- *Setup.* Field dimensions and equipment needs are listed under this heading. Balls, cones, flags, and colored scrimmage vests are some of the most common equipment items. When field dimensions are listed they are provided only as general guidelines, and should be adjusted to the number and ability of players.

- *Procedure.* This section provides a brief description of how the game is played. Coaches may call fouls and act as servers or scorekeepers while observing the action. The games are designed so that players can use their own initiative and decision-making powers to organize the games and get play started.

- *Scoring.* When appropriate, a scoring system has been provided to add an element of competition to the game. It should be clearly understood, however, that the ultimate aim of each game is for players to challenge themelves to achieve a higher standard of performance. Improvement is the true barometer of success, not who wins or loses the competition.

- *Practice Tips.* These are provided to help coaches (or players) organize the games in the most efficient and effective manner. Most deal with the skills or tactics involved, with possible adjustments in the size of the playing area, and with restrictions that can be placed upon the players (for instance, one- or two-touch passing). Safety and liability concerns are also addressed. For example, separate groups of players should not be positioned so that players from one group may inadvertently run into the space occupied by another group.

Planning Practice Sessions

These guidelines apply to players of all ages and ability levels and are provided to help coaches plan their practice sessions.

Consider the Players. Plan a realistic practice, one that challenges players but also is within their physical and mental limits. Consider your players' ages, abilities, and developmental level. Beginning players may have difficulty executing even fundamental skills, so it is important that coaches do not place them in situations where they have little or no chance of achieving success.

Develop a Theme. Each practice should have a central underlying theme. For example, the primary objective of a session might be to improve passing and receiving skills, or to create goal-scoring opportunities through creative dribbling. Organize the practice around a variety of exercises and games related to the central theme. It is usually a mistake to try to cover too many different topics in a single session, particularly with younger players.

Coach in a Progressive Manner. Each drill or exercise used in a practice session should provide a foundation for those that follow. Begin with basic activities and gradually progress to matchlike situations. For example, a practice might begin with simple passing drills involving little or no player movement and gradually progress to exercises where players pass and receive the ball while competing against opponents. Where to start in the progression depends upon the ability and experience of the players. Higher-level players should naturally begin with more demanding drills than novice players. In both cases, however, organize the drills so that each serves as a natural lead-in for the next.

Keep Players Active. Maximize time on task. The more times a player can pass, receive, shoot, or dribble the ball during a practice, the more he or she will improve skills and enjoy the session. Make sure that a large supply of balls, ideally one for each player, is available. The easiest way to guarantee this is to require each player to bring a ball to practice. Just as baseball players bring their glove to the field, soccer players should bring a ball. An ample supply of balls provides the coach many more options with regard to his or her choice of drills and practice games, and makes training more enjoyable for the players since they have the opportunity to touch the ball more often.

Make Practice FUN! Conduct a boring practice and you create a poor learning environment. Through careful planning and creative thinking coaches can develop stimulating, fun-filled training sessions that will achieve their learning objectives. The practice games described in this book will help you do this.

Keep It Simple. Much of soccer's inherent beauty is its simplicity. Avoid complicated drills or exercises which usually serve only to confuse and frustrate players. In soccer circles this is often referred to as the "KISS" principle—"Keep it simple, stupid!"

Don't Overcoach. Practice should be centered around the players, not the coaches. Use brief demonstrations, simple explanations, and then get the players actively involved. Stop an exercise to provide specific feedback only when an opportune time to make a coaching point occurs.

Provide a Safe Environment. Because soccer is a contact sport, it involves a certain amount of physical risk. Accidental collisions, bruises, and bumps will sometimes occur. To minimize injuries, the coach must make every effort to provide players with a safe practice environment. This includes adequate supervision and planning, matching players with others of similar size and ability, and establishing guidelines for appropriate behavior.

It is also essential that players wear appropriate equipment during practice and games. All players should wear shin guards that help to prevent serious injury to the lower legs. Most guards are made of light, flexible plastic and are relatively inexpensive. Goalkeepers should wear padded shorts or padded pants, particularly when playing on hard natural surfaces or artificial turf. Two common styles are knee-length "knickers" and full-length pants. Both have padding over the hip area, and the long pants also have protective padding around the knees.

Use care in selecting soccer goals. Homemade portable goals (8 feet high by 24 feet wide) can topple over despite their heavy weight if they are not properly anchored, if they are moved, and if youngsters play on them rambunctiously. Solid, professionally made goals are expensive, but you can substitute cones, flags, or other kinds of markers if cost makes them prohibitive or if you want to set up practice games in several areas.

Employ Economical Training Methods. Incorporate the elements of fitness, skill and/or tactics into each exercise to make the most effective use of practice time. Towards that aim coaches should include a ball in every drill or exercise, even those designed primarily to improve fitness.

End with a Match. End each practice with a match or a simulated match situation. The match need not be full-sided (11 vs. 11). Small-sided matches (3 vs. 3 up to 7 vs. 7) are actually more beneficial in many respects. Playing with fewer numbers per team allows players the opportunity to touch the ball more often. They are also required to make more decisions, which aids their tactical development. In small-sided matches the emphasis on positional play is greatly reduced since each player must defend as well as attack, a situation that promotes overall player development. Last but not least, the number of scoring chances is greatly increased, and this makes the matches more fun for everyone.

Part I

GAMES FOR WARM-UP AND CONDITIONING

Warm-up exercises raise muscle temperatures, promote increased blood flow and oxygen supply, improve muscular contraction and reflex time, and prevent muscle strains and soreness the next day. Players should warm up at sufficient intensity to cause sweating, which indicates that muscle temperatures have been elevated. This may take anywhere from 15 to 30 minutes depending upon the temperature, humidity, and general environmental conditions surrounding the practice setting.

The traditional warm-up includes a variety of stretching activities as well as old standard exercises such as jumping jacks, sit-ups, push-ups, and knee bends. While there is nothing wrong with those exercises, they certainly won't generate excitement and enthusiasm in young players. The games described in this part are designed to add variety and spice to the warm-up. Skill development is an added benefit inasmuch as most games involve the use of one or more balls. Player conditioning can also be maintained and developed in part through the games described in this section.

Essential components of soccer fitness include flexibility or range of motion, agility and mobility, aerobic and anaerobic endurance, and muscular strength and power. Speed is also an important consideration. Players can develop soccer-specific speed through warm-up exercises involving sudden changes of speed and direction coupled with deceptive feinting movements. Quickness, and the ability to change direction quickly, are just as important to a soccer player as straight-out sprinting speed.

1

Dancing Feet

Minutes: 10-15   **Players:**   Unlimited (pairs)

Objective: Practice one- and two-touch passing skills in a warm-up activity

Setup: Using markers, outline a rectangular area 30 by 40 yards. Pair players with partners, giving each pair a ball. Station all pairs within the field area with partners about 2 to 3 yards apart.

Procedure: Partners pass the ball back and forth, using the inside or outside surface of the feet, as they move throughout the area. They should move continuously once the round begins—stationary passing is not permitted. Partners try to maintain a distance of 2 to 3 yards while moving and passing. Allow only one- and two-touch passing. Play 10 to 15 rounds of 1 minute each, with a short break after each.

Scoring: Each pair keeps count of how many passes it completes in a round. The pair completing the most passes receives 2 points; the second-place pair gets 1 point. The pair scoring the most points after all rounds wins.

Practice Tips: Passing accuracy, close control of the ball, and good field vision are critical for successful performance. Players should use one-touch passing when possible. The size of the playing area depends on the number of players, their ages, and their ability. Ten to 12 pairs can comfortably play in a 30- by 40-yard area. Enlarge the area for more pairs.

2

Juggling Competition

Minutes: 5-10   **Players:**   Unlimited (groups of 3)

Objectives: Warm muscles before more vigorous training and improve ball control

Setup: Using markers, outline a rectangular area 10 by 15 yards for each group. Each group has a ball.

Procedure: Players try to keep the ball airborne using feet, thighs, chest, and head, but not arms and hands. Allow a maximum of three touches of the ball before it is passed.

Scoring: Assess 1 penalty point to any player who allows the ball to drop to the ground, or causes the ball to leave the playing area. Player with the least penalty points wins.

Practice Tips: The key elements required for skillful ball control are confidence, concentration, and proper technique. Beginners often lack confidence and as a result are often too rigid and tense. Encourage players to relax and withdraw the receiving surface of the body as the ball arrives. This cushions the impact of the ball and keeps it within close control. The game can be made more difficult by reducing the number of touches allowed or by requiring players to juggle while jogging around the area.

3

Nutmeg Competition

Minutes: 10 (two 5-minute periods)

Players: Unlimited (two equal teams)

Objective: Warm muscles and prepare the body for more vigorous training; improve ability to dribble in confined area

Setup: Using markers, outline a rectangular area 25 by 30 yards. Position Team 1 players randomly within the area as stationary targets with feet 2 to 3 feet apart. Station Team 2 players, each with a ball, outside the area.

Procedure: Team 2 players dribble into the area and attempt to pass the ball through the legs of as many opponents as possible during a 5-minute period. (This maneuver is known as "nutmeg.") Opponents must remain stationary, with feet planted. A dribbler may not nutmeg the same opponent twice in succession. Teams reverse roles for the second round.

Scoring: Each player counts the number of nutmegs he or she accomplishes. Individual totals are combined for the team score. Team scoring highest total wins.

Practice Tips: Adjust the playing area to the number of players. Encourage dribblers to keep their heads up as much as possible to ensure optimal field vision.

4

Round-the-Circle Dribble

Minutes: 10   **Players:** 6-10 (two equal teams)

Objectives: Improve fitness and dribbling speed

Setup: Using markers, outline a circle 20 to 25 yards in diameter. Pair each player with a partner from the opposing team. Number each pair. Position players on the perimeter directly across the circle from their partner. One player in each pair has a ball.

Procedure: Begin by calling a pair number, for example "Number 3's." These two players immediately sprint counterclockwise around the perimeter of the circle, the one with the ball dribbling and the other pursuing. The dribbler's aim is to go right round the circle before being tagged by the partner. As soon as the players return to their original positions call a different numbered pair. Continue by calling pairs in random order. Partners exchange possession of the ball after each circuit.

Scoring: Team gets 1 point when the dribbler completes a circuit before being tagged. Team scoring the most points wins.

Practice Tips: Adjust the circle size to the age and ability of players. The circumference should give the chaser a reasonable chance of catching the dribbler. Vary by requiring the dribbler to make two circuits without being tagged.

5

Round-the-Flag Relay

Minutes: 15   **Players:**   Unlimited (equal teams of 5-7)

Objectives: Develop dribbling speed and improve fitness

Setup: Use the sideline or end line of the field as a starting line. Position teams side by side in single file behind the starting line. Keep teams at least 3 yards apart. Place a flag or cone 25 yards directly in front of each team. The first player in each line has a ball.

Procedure: On the command "Go," the first player in each line dribbles as fast as possible around the marker and back to the starting line, where he or she surrenders the ball to the second player. All players dribble the circuit in turn. The team completing the relay in the shortest time wins. Repeat 10 times, with a short rest between each race.

Scoring: Team completing the relay first gets 1 point. Team scoring the most points in 10 races wins.

Practice Tips: The technique used when dribbling in open space differs from that used when dribbling in a crowd of players. Rather than keeping the ball under close control, players should push it several steps ahead and then sprint to catch up to it. Adjust the distance covered to the age and fitness of players.

6

Leapfrog Races

Minutes: 5-10   **Players:** Unlimited (teams of 3-5)

Objectives: Develop upper body strength and muscular endurance; develop leg strength and power

Setup: Using markers, indicate a starting line and a finishing line 50 yards apart. Teammates position in single file behind the starting line. Keep teams at least 5 yards apart. The first player in each line leans forward at the waist and crouches with knees flexed and hands placed slightly above the knees.

Procedure: On the coach's command "Go," the second player in each line places his or her hands on #1's upper back and leapfrogs upward and over and then crouches a little ahead of #1. Player #3 leapfrogs over players #1 and #2, and so on. Players continue leapfrogging to the finish line.

Scoring: First team to place all players across the finish line wins. Run five races.

Practice Tips: Leapfrog races are more suitable for more mature players with the required upper body and leg strength. For children 12 years and under, shorten the distance to decrease the physical demands of the game. In addition to developing muscular strength, leapfrog races generate laughter and enjoyment among players.

7

Across-the-Circle Run

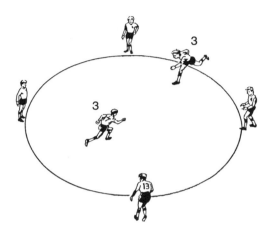

Minutes: 5-10 **Players:** Two equal teams of 3-5

Objectives: Improve running speed and develop endurance

Setup: Using markers, outline a circle 20 to 25 yards in diameter. Pair each player with an opponent. Number each pair. Position partners directly opposite each other on the perimeter of the circle.

Procedure: Call out a pair number, for example, "Number 3." These players immediately change position by sprinting across the circle. The aim is to arrive at the opponent's space before he or she arrives at your space. The coach calls on pairs in random order. Two pairs may be called upon at the same time.

Scoring: Player who arrives first at his or her opponent's space scores 1 team point. Team scoring the most points wins.

Practice Tips: Adjust the size of the circle to the physical capabilities of the players. For players 12 and under reduce the diameter to 10 to 15 yards. Vary by requiring players to run across the circle and then back to their original spots.

8

3-Line Shuffle

Minutes: 5   **Players:**   Unlimited (three equal teams)

Objectives: Warm muscles prior to more vigorous activity and improve mobility and agility

Setup: Position teams side by side in single-file columns facing the coach. Allow 5 yards between the columns, which are numbered 1, 2, and 3.

Procedure: Players must instantly respond to the commands of the coach, who may choose from three options. If the coach calls "Number 1!" Columns 1 and 2 switch positions, using a sideways shuffle movement of the feet. If the coach calls "Number 2!" Columns 2 and 3 change places. If the coach calls "Number 3!" Columns 1 and 3 change places. Issue commands in random order so players cannot anticipate the direction of their next movement. Players assume the number of the column space to which they have moved after changing positions.

Scoring: A player who moves in the wrong direction, or to the wrong space, is assessed 1 penalty point. Team tallying the least number of penalty points wins.

Practice Tips: Players must use a side-shuffle movement, without crossing their legs. They must take care not to collide with other players. Success at this game depends upon mental concentration as well as quick reactions and proper footwork.

9

Hounds and Hares

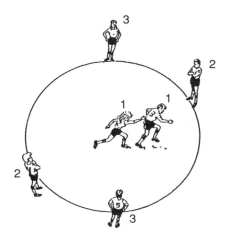

Minutes: 3-8 (3 to 5 rounds of 60 to 90 seconds for each pair)

Players: 6-8 (in pairs)

Objectives: Improve mobility, agility, and fitness

Setup: Using markers, outline a circle 20 to 25 yards in diameter. Number each pair. Position partners on the perimeter of the circle directly opposite each other.

Procedure: Call out a pair number, for example, "Number 1," who enter the circle. Designate one of the pair as the "hound," who immediately gives chase and attempts to tag his or her partner (the "hare"). Once the hare is tagged, roles immediately reverse. After 60 to 90 seconds call a different pair into the circle, and so on.

Scoring: Player tagged the fewest times wins.

Practice Tips: The "hare" should use quick changes of speed and direction to elude the "hound." Make the game more physically challenging by lengthening the time of each round or by increasing the size of the circle. As a variation call two or three pairs into the circle at the same time.

10

Chain Tag

Minutes: 5-10   **Players:** Unlimited

Objectives: Improve mobility, agility, and endurance

Setup: Using markers, outline a rectangular area 30 by 35 yards. Designate 2 players as "it" and position them outside the area. Station all remaining "free" players within the area.

Procedure: The "it" players enter the area to chase after and tag "free" players. A free player who is tagged must join hands with the player who tagged him or her to form a chain. The original chains may not split into smaller chains when attempting to catch free players; only two chains are permitted at any one time. Chains can work together to corner or trap free players. Players must remain in the area. Repeat the game as necessary for 5 to 10 minutes.

Scoring: Longest chain at the end of the game wins.

Practice Tips: Vary the size of the area, or the number of chains allowed, depending upon the number of players. Free players should use sudden changes of speed and direction coupled with deceptive body feints to avoid being tagged.

11

Circle Pinball

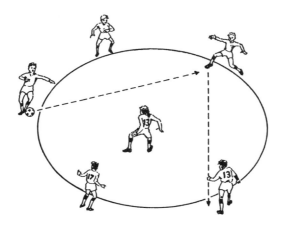

Minutes: 10-15   **Players:** 5-8

Objective: Warm up players prior to vigorous training and develop one-touch passing technique

Setup: Using markers, outline a circle about 30 feet in diameter. Station a defender within the circle; position all other players (attackers) an equal distance apart outside the circle, along the perimeter. One attacker has a ball.

Procedure: Attackers attempt to keep possession of the ball from the defender by interpassing across the circle. They are allowed to move along the perimeter of the circle to receive passes but are not permitted to enter the circle. Attackers may pass to any teammate but must use one-touch passes only. If the ball goes out of the circle, or if the defender intercepts a pass, the ball is immediately returned to one of the attackers and the game continues.

Scoring: Attackers get 1 point for 8 consecutive passes without loss of possession. Defender gets 1 point each time he or she intercepts a pass or causes an attacker to use more than one touch to play the ball. For each time the ball goes out of the circle, the defender also scores 1 point. Play to a score of 10, then switch defenders.

Practice Tips: Enlarge the size of the circle or allow two-touch passing for less skilled players. Position two defenders in the circle to make the game more challenging for attackers.

12

Hunt the Fox

Minutes: 10-15   **Players:**   Two equal teams of 6-10

Objectives: Develop endurance and practice positioning for combination passing

Setup: Using markers, outline a rectangular area about 40 by 50 yards; station both teams within it. Colored scrimmage vests differentiate teams. Designate one player on each team as a "fox" who should wear distinctive clothing. Each team has a ball.

Procedure: Passing is accomplished by throwing and catching—not kicking—the ball. The objective is to hit the opposing fox below the knees with a thrown ball. A player may take only five steps with the ball before passing to a teammate or throwing at the fox. Teammates can protect their fox by blocking or deflecting opponents' throws. Change of possession occurs when a pass is intercepted by a member of the opposing team, the ball drops to the ground, or a player takes too many steps with the ball. Players should call the fouls. Keep two balls in play at all times.

Scoring: Team gets 1 point each time a player hits the opposing fox; the team scoring the most points wins.

Practice Tips: Emphasize quick, short passes that are likely to be completed. Players should continually reposition to provide passing options for the teammate with the ball.

13

Piggyback Soccer

Minutes: 15   **Players:** Two equal teams of 10-14

Objectives: Develop leg strength and muscular endurance

Setup: Using markers, outline a rectangular area 25 by 40 yards. Position a goal 3 yards wide at the center of each end line. Pair each player with a teammate of comparable size and weight. Colored scrimmage vests differentiate teams. One team has a ball.

Procedure: Begin with a kickoff from the center of the field. Each team defends a goal and tries to score in the opponents' goal. There are no goalkeepers. Each player must carry his or her partner piggyback fashion during play. Partners change position every 30 to 60 seconds to share the burden of carrying each other. Otherwise regular soccer rules apply.

Scoring: Goals are scored by kicking the ball through the opponent's goal below waist height. Team scoring the most goals wins.

Practice Tips: Avoid physical mismatches between partners. This game is most appropriate for players of high school and college age; it is not suitable for young players who lack sufficient strength and coordination. Use good judgment!

14

Dribble to Safety

Minutes: 10   **Players:** Unlimited

Objectives: Develop passing and dribbling skills in a warm-up activity

Setup: Using markers, outline a rectangular area about 20 by 35 yards, with a safety zone 5 yards wide at each end. Station two or three "marksmen" in the center of the field, with balls. All remaining players, each with a ball, station in one of the safety zones.

Procedure: Players in the safety zone attempt to dribble the length of the field. Marksmen can prevent dribblers from reaching the opposite safety zone by contacting them with a passed ball. All passes must be made with the inside or outside surface of the foot. Marksmen can move about the area by dribbling. A player trying to reach a safety zone who is contacted below the waist with a passed ball, or who loses control of his or her ball outside the field boundaries, is considered captured and becomes a marksman. Dribblers who reach the safety zone remain there until the coach commands them to dribble back to the other safety zone. Players dribble between safety zones until all have become marksmen.

Scoring: Last dribbler to elude the marksmen wins.

Practice Tips: Adjust the area to the ages, abilities, and number of players. Encourage the marksmen to dribble close to their targets before passing the ball.

15

Escape From the Crab Monsters

Minutes: 5 (repeated)   **Players:** Unlimited

Objectives: Develop dribbling skills

Setup: Using markers, outline a rectangular area 15 by 25 yards. Designate 5 or 6 players as "crabs," and station them within the area. They must move about in the "crab" posture, a sitting position with weight supported by the hands and feet. All remaining players, each with a ball, station outside the area.

Procedure: Players dribble into the area. The crabs chase the dribblers and try to kick the balls out of the area. Crabs must remain in the crab position and not use hands to play the ball. Crabs can work together to force dribblers into making mistakes. Dribblers should use quick changes of speed and direction, coupled with deceptive body feints, to elude the crabs. A dribbler whose ball is kicked out of the area should quickly retrieve it and return to the game. Repeat the game several times using different players as crabs for each game.

Scoring: Crabs get 1 point for each ball kicked out of the area. Crab totaling the most points wins.

Practice Tips: Decrease the area or increase the number of crabs to make the game more challenging for dribblers. Caution players not to step on a crab's hands.

16

Dribble Freeze Tag

Minutes: 3 per round (several rounds)   **Players:**   Unlimited

Objectives: Practice dribbling skills in a warm-up activity

Setup: Using markers, outline a rectangular area 25 by 30 yards. Designate 2 players as "it" and position them outside the area, without balls. Station remaining players, each with a ball, within the area.

Procedure: Players begin dribbling randomly within the area. At the coach's command, the "it" players enter the area to chase and tag the dribblers. A dribbler who is tagged is considered "frozen" and must sit on his or her ball. Free dribblers can release those who are frozen by dribbling close and touching them on the shoulder. Repeat the game several times with different players designated as "it."

Scoring: A player who is "it" gets 1 point for each dribbler that he or she tags. The "it" player who freezes the most dribblers wins the round.

Practice Tips: Adjust the size of the playing area to the ages and number of players. Older players often require more space than younger players.

17

Team Tag

Minutes: 10-15   **Players:** Four equal teams of 4-6

Objectives: Develop dribbling skills in a warm-up activity

Setup: Using markers, outline a rectangular area 25 by 40 yards. Station all teams within the area. Designate one team as "it." Colored scrimmage vests distinguish teams. Each player has a ball.

Procedure: Players from the "it" team dribble after players from the other teams and attempt to tag them with a hand. All players must dribble a ball throughout the exercise. Players who are tagged are eliminated from the game and must leave the playing area. They practice ball juggling on their own until the game is completed. Continue until all players have been eliminated. Play four games, designating a different team as "it" for each game.

Scoring: Team tagging all its opponents in the least time wins. Coach keeps time.

Practice Tips: Reduce the playing area for younger players. As a variation, allow players on the "it" team to chase without dribbling.

18

Crabs and Fishes

Minutes: 10-15   **Players:**   Unlimited

Objectives: Improve dribbling skills in a warm-up activity

Setup: Using markers, outline a rectangular area 20 by 30 yards, with a safety zone 3 yards wide at each end. Designate 3 players as "crabs" and station them, without a ball, in the center of the area. Crabs assume a sitting position, with the body off the ground, supported by their arms and legs. All remaining players are "fishes" and are stationed in one of the safety zones, each with a ball.

Procedure: On the coach's signal "Go," the fish attempt to dribble from one safety zone into the other. The crabs try to steal and then kick the balls out of the playing area. A fish whose ball is kicked out of the area retrieves the ball and practices ball juggling until the game has ended. Crabs must remain in the "crab" position and may not use hands to play the ball. Fish who dribble from one safety zone to the other remain there until the coach commands them to dribble back to the original safety zone. Fish continue dribbling from one safety zone to the other until only three remain. Designate these players as "crabs" to begin the next game.

Scoring: None

Practice Tips: Dribblers must not chip the ball over the crabs. In this exercise the dribblers must try to penetrate through a line of defenders (crabs) on their way to the goal (safety zone). Reduce the width of the area to make the game more challenging for the dribblers.

19

Crab Soccer

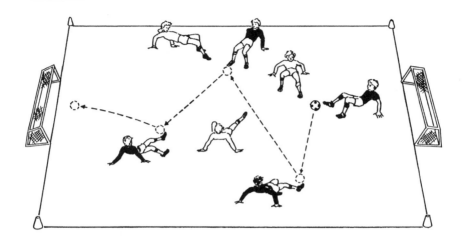

Minutes: 15   **Players:** Equal teams of 5-8

Objectives: Develop muscular strength and power in arms, chest, and legs

Setup: Using markers, outline a rectangular area 20 by 35 yards. Place a goal 3 yards wide at the center of each end line. Colored scrimmage vests differentiate teams. One team has a ball.

Procedure: Begin with a kickoff from the center of the field. Each team defends a goal and attempts to score in the opponents' goal. There are no goalkeepers. Players must remain in the crab posture, a sitting position with the body slightly elevated off the ground by arms and legs when moving about the field. Otherwise regular soccer rules apply.

Scoring: Team that scores the most goals wins.

Practice Tips: Encourage players to keep their bodies elevated off the ground as much as possible to increase the strength training benefits of the game. When fatigued they can sit for a moment for a rest. Crab soccer provides a fun change from traditional warm-up.

20

6-Zone Game

Minutes: 15   **Players:**   Two teams of 9

Objectives: Develop dribbling and tackling skills in a warm-up session

Setup: Using markers, outline a rectangular area about 40 by 60 yards. Divide the area lengthwise with markers into six equal zones numbered 1 though 6. Team A positions 4 players in Zone #2, 3 players in Zone #4, and 2 players in Zone #6. Zones #1, #3, and #5 are neutral, without players. Team B players, each with a ball, position on the end line nearer Zone #1.

Procedure: Team B players try to dribble the length of the area without losing possession of the ball. Defending (Team A) players attempt to steal balls from the dribblers while staying within their respective zones. Defending players must use the block tackle to gain possession of the ball. Do not permit them to use the slide tackle or enter the neutral zones. Repeat the game 10 times (teams switch positions after each round).

Scoring: Each player who dribbles the length of the field without losing possession scores 1 team point. Team scoring the most points in 10 games wins.

Practice Tips: Adjust the size of the area to the ability of the players. Challenge skilled players by reducing the area, and give novices a larger one. The slide tackle is prohibited for safety.

Part II

GAMES FOR SKILL TRAINING

Soccer players must develop the skills used to pass, receive, head, dribble, shield, and shoot the ball. The ultimate aim of skill training is that players be able to transfer what they learn in practice to match play. As the saying goes, however, you must learn to walk before you are able to run. Introduce skills in a relatively pressure-free learning environment where young players will experience some degree of success. Training can then progress to more challenging situations involving the match-related pressures of movement, limited space, restricted time, and determined opponents.

The practice games described in this part are grouped according to the skills they emphasize. Within each group the games have been ordered so that each successive game demands slightly more of players. Coaches can also create varying degrees of difficulty within the same game. Reducing the available space, increasing the speed of repetition, or limiting the number of touches players can use to control the ball makes each game more challenging for players.

Passing and Receiving Skills

21

Soccer Golf

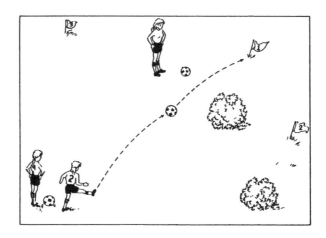

Minutes: 20-30   **Players:**   Unlimited (groups of 3)

Objectives: Develop the ability to kick a ball accurately for varying distances

Setup: Play on a regulation-size field or larger. Position 9 to 18 flagposts or cones at various locations to represent holes. Each player has a ball.

Procedure: Players can compete individually within their group or collectively as a team against another 3-player team. Each player tees off with a placekick from a designated starting point (tee). The basic rules of golf apply except that the ball is kicked with the instep or side of the foot rather than stroked with a club. The ball must hit a flagpost or cone to be considered to be in the hole. Players take turns, moving from hole to hole over the entire course. Schedule group tee off times 5 minutes apart if several teams are playing at once.

Scoring: Player (or team) completing the course with the least number of kicks wins.

Practice Tips: Soccer golf requires concentration and proper skill execution, but not much physical effort. Play this game on the day after a match, when players may be tired, sore, and stiff. For variation specify the type of pass that must be used, or limit all kicks to the player's weaker foot. Fitness training can be added by having players sprint to the ball after each kick.

22

Pass Through the Tunnel

Minutes: 10

Players: Unlimited (in pairs)

Objectives: Improve passing skills

Setup: Play within a rectangular area 40 by 60 yards. Each pair has a ball.

Procedure: Partners position side by side within the area. To begin the game the player without the ball jogs 10 to 20 yards from his or her partner, and positions with feet spread to form a tunnel. The partner attempts to pass a ball through the tunnel. After each pass the "tunnel" jogs to a different area of the field and repositions. His or her partner collects the ball and attempts to pass through the new tunnel. Players switch roles after 30 passes.

Scoring: Each pass that goes through the tunnel scores 1 point. Player scoring the most points wins.

Practice Tips: Beginners should practice short passes (5-10 yards), and experienced players practice longer passes (20 yards or more). You may place restrictions on the type of pass to be used. For example, the inside-of-foot pass is the most effective technique over short distances of 10 to 15 yards, whereas the instep pass is more appropriate for distances greater than 20 yards.

23

Partner Chip

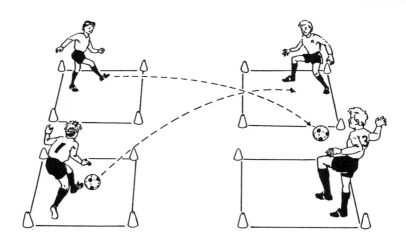

Minutes:　10-15　　　　　　　　**Players:**　Unlimited (groups of 2)

Objectives:　Develop the ability to accurately chip (loft) passes

Setup:　Pair players for competition. Using markers, outline two squares 5 by 5 yards, positioned 15 to 25 yards apart for each pair. One partner stations in each square. Each pair has a ball.

Procedure:　Partners chip the ball back and forth between squares. Each player attempts 30 lofted passes.

Scoring:　A chip pass that drops directly into a square gains 2 points. A pass that bounces into a square on one hop gains 1 point. Partner who gains the most points wins.

Practice Tips:　Adjust the distance between squares and the size of the squares to the ages and abilities of the players. Allow beginning players to pass the ball with their favorite foot, but require advanced players to alternate passing with right and left feet.

24

Monkey in the Middle

Minutes: 10-15   **Players:** Unlimited (groups of 3)

Objectives: Develop the ability to loft (chip) passes over opponents

Setup: Using markers, outline a rectangular area 10 by 30 yards, divided into three 10 by 10-yard zones. Position one player in each zone. Each group has a ball.

Procedure: Players stationed in the end zones attempt to chip the ball back and forth over the player in the middle zone. Players are limited to two touches of the ball—the first to control and the second to pass. The middle player tries to intercept passes by moving within the central zone to front the passer and block the passing lane.

Scoring: Players in the end zones compete against the middle player. Each chip pass from one end zone into the other gains 2 points. Penalize players in the end zones 1 point if they use more than two touches to control and return the ball, and 1 point if the ball leaves the playing area. Give the middle player 1 point for each pass interception. Player(s) scoring most points wins. Play game to 20 points, then repeat with all players moving into a different zone.

Practice Tips: Players should use a short, powerful motion of the kicking leg to chip the ball. Imparting slight backspin by driving the instep underneath the ball will make the passed ball easier to receive and control. This game is not appropriate for novices who have not mastered basic passing skills.

25

Toss, Receive, and Catch

Minutes: 15   **Players:**   8-12 (two equal teams)

Objectives: Improve ability to receive and control balls out of the air and develop endurance

Setup: Using markers, outline a rectangular area 30 by 40 yards and position all players within it. Colored scrimmage vests differentiate teams. One team has the ball.

Procedure: The team with the ball plays "keepaway" from its opponents. Passing is accomplished by throwing and catching. Players must receive and control each toss using their instep, thigh, chest, or head, and then catch the ball with their hands before it drops to the ground. Players may take up to five steps while in possession of the ball before passing to a teammate. The defending team gains possession by intercepting passes, or when an opponent fails to control the ball before it drops to the ground. Players are not permitted to wrestle the ball away from opponents.

Scoring: Team gets 1 point for 10 consecutive passes. The team scoring the most points wins.

Practice Tips: Players should withdraw the receiving surface of the body as the ball arrives, to cushion the impact. Adjust the size of the area to the number of players. This game may not be appropriate for players who have not mastered fundamental receiving skills.

26

Passing by the Numbers

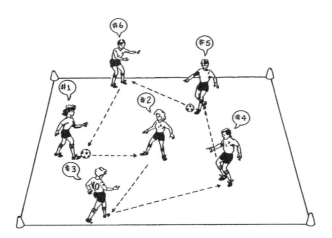

Minutes: 10-15 **Players:** Unlimited (groups of 6-8)

Objectives: Develop passing and receiving skills and improve endurance

Setup: Using markers, outline a rectangular area about 30 by 40 yards for each group and position each group in an area. Number the players in each group, beginning with #1 and continuing up through the number of players in the group. Give 2 players in each group possession of a ball to begin the game.

Procedure: All players begin jogging within the area, the two with a ball dribbling it. Those with a ball locate the teammate numbered directly above and pass to him or her. (The player with the highest number passes to #1.) All players should move continuously during the exercise as they pass to the teammate numbered above them and receive passes from the teammate numbered below them.

Scoring: None

Practice Tips: Encourage players to pass and receive the ball in a smooth, controlled manner. The ball should never be completely stopped; rather, it should be received and controlled in the direction of the player's next movement. Make the game more challenging by placing restrictions on players (for example, require them to pass only with their weakest foot, or pass only with either the outside or instep surface of the foot).

27

Soccer Dodge Ball

Minutes: Play until all players are eliminated (usually about 3-5 minutes per game).

Players: Two equal teams of 6-12

Objectives: Improve passing skills; improve dribbling skills; develop agility, mobility, and fitness

Setup: Using markers, outline a rectangular area 25 by 35 yards. Team A is stationed within the area, without a ball. Team B players, each with a ball, station outside the area.

Procedure: Team B players dribble into the area and try to pass the ball to hit Team A players below the knees. All passes must be made with the inside or outside surface of the foot. Team A players may move anywhere within the area to avoid being hit by a ball. Any player hit with a ball below the knees is eliminated. He or she must then go outside the area and may practice individual ball juggling until the game is completed.

Scoring: Team eliminating all its opponents in the shortest time wins. Repeat the game several times, with teams switching roles each time.

Practice Tips: Emphasize passing accuracy rather than power. Encourage players to dribble as close as possible to their intended targets before passing the ball. Adjust the playing area to the ages and abilities of players.

28

Join the Hunt

Minutes: 10-15   **Players:**   10-20

Objectives: Improve passing and dribbling skills; develop agility and mobility

Setup: Using markers, outline a rectangular area about 30 by 40 yards. Designate 2 or 3 players as "hunters," who station outside the area, each with a ball. All other players station within the area without balls. Position a supply of balls, one for each player, just outside the area.

Procedure: The hunters enter the area to dribble after and contact "free" players below the knees with a passed ball. Free players may move anywhere within the area to avoid being hit. A player hit by a passed ball below the knees becomes a hunter. Continue until all free players have joined the hunt. Repeat the game several times, choosing different players as hunters to begin each game.

Scoring: None

Practice Tips: Adjust the area to the ages, abilities, and number of players. Encourage hunters to dribble close to their targets before passing, to help develop dribbling skills. Place restrictions on players to emphasize a specific type of pass (for example, use only inside-of-foot or instep passes). As a variation require that all players pass with their weakest foot.

29

Chase the Rabbit

Minutes: 15 (or 10 points, whichever comes first)

Players: Unlimited (three equal teams)

Objectives: Improve passing accuracy; develop combination passing; develop endurance

Setup: Using markers, outline a rectangular area about 30 by 40 yards. Station all three teams in the playing area. Designate one player on each team as a "rabbit," who should wear a distinctive shirt or hat. Colored scrimmage vests differentiate teams. Each team has two balls.

Procedure: Players attempt to contact the opposing team's "rabbit" below the waist with a ball. Rabbits try to elude their opponents and avoid getting hit with a ball. They can do so by employing sudden changes of speed and direction. Teammates attempt to move the ball into position to hit the opponent's rabbit through good communication and quick, precise passing combinations.

Scoring: Player contacting a rabbit with a passed ball below the waist gets 1 point. Teams keep total of their points scored. First team to total 10 points (or team with the highest number of points after 15 minutes) wins.

Practice Tips: Emphasize accuracy rather than power. Adjust the total number of points required to win to the ages and abilities of players. Reduce the area for younger, less skilled players.

30

4-Zone Passing Game

Minutes: 10-15   **Players:**   Two teams of 6

Objectives: Improve passing accuracy and practice proper support positioning of players near the ball

Setup: Using markers, outline a rectangular area 20 by 40 yards. Divide the area into four 20 by 10-yard zones, numbered consecutively #1, #2, #3, and #4. Position 3 players from Team A in Zone #1 and 3 players in Zone #3. Position 3 players from Team B in Zones #2 and #4, respectively. Each team has a ball.

Procedure: The objective is for players in one zone to pass their ball through the adjoining zone to teammates in the next zone. All passes must travel below waist height. Opposing players try to intercept passes traveling through their zone. Teams lose possession of their ball if a pass is intercepted or if they kick the ball out of the playing area. All players must remain in their assigned zone throughout the game.

Scoring: Team gets 1 point for each pass completed to a teammate in the other zone. The team scoring the most points wins.

Practice Tips: Teammates may pass among themselves within their zone until they can find gaps between opponents in the adjoining zone through which they can pass the ball. Restrictions, such as requiring two-touch passing only, can be imposed to make the game more challenging for advanced players.

31

Game With Targets

Minutes: 15-20   **Players:**   Two equal teams of 5-7

Objectives: Develop team play through combination passing, proper support movement, and off-the-ball running

Setup: Play in one half of a regulation field. Designate a "target" player for each team, with a distinctive colored vest or a hat. One team has the ball.

Procedure: Begin with a kickoff from the center of the field. Teammates try to keep the ball from opponents and also try to complete passes to their target player. Change of possession occurs when a defending player intercepts a pass, when the ball travels out of the area, or after a point has been scored. Regular soccer rules apply, except for the method of scoring.

Scoring: Team gets 1 point for six consecutive passes and 2 points for a pass completed to team's "target" player. Team scoring the most points wins.

Practice Tips: Reduce the area for highly skilled players. As a variation designate two target players on each team.

32

Perimeter Passing Game

Minutes: 30   **Players:**   9 (three teams of 3)

Objectives: Develop interpassing and team support; develop concepts of defensive pressure, cover, and balance

Setup: Using markers, outline a rectangular area about 30 by 40 yards; station one team in the center as defenders. Players from the other teams station along the perimeter as attackers. One attacker has the ball.

Procedure: The attacking players work together to keep the ball from the defending team. They may move side to side along the perimeter to support teammates or receive passes but must remain close to the perimeter line. The attackers are also limited to three touches for receiving and passing the ball. Defenders may move about anywhere within the area. A defending player who steals the ball returns it immediately to an attacker to continue play. Each team plays one 10-minute period as defenders (and two as attackers).

Scoring: Defending team gets 1 point for each steal and for when the attacking team loses the ball outside the playing area. Attacking team gets 1 point for 8 consecutive passes without loss of ball. Best total on defense and attack wins.

Practice Tips: Defending players should work together to limit the attackers' options and reduce passing space. Attacking players should pass the ball quickly between areas (changing the point of attack) to prevent defenders from closing the space and gaining the ball. Adjust the playing area to the ages and abilities of players. The smaller the area, the easier it is for the defending team.

33

Zone Soccer Game

Minutes: 20-25   **Players:** Two teams of 3

Objectives: Develop passing combinations and improve ability to attack and defend in small groups

Setup: Using markers, outline rectangular area 50 by 25 yards. Designate two end zones 10 yards deep spanning the width of the field, one for each team. Station both teams in the central area of the field between the end zones. There are no goals or goalkeepers.

Procedure: Begin with a kickoff from the center of the field. Basic soccer rules apply, except that players score by completing a pass to a teammate in the opponents' end zone. A pass is completed when the teammate receives and controls the ball. Defending players may not enter their end zone to intercept passes; they must try to prevent passes from entering their end zone. Change of possession occurs when the defending team steals the ball, when the ball goes out of play last touched by a member of the attacking team, or after a completed pass to a teammate in the opponents' zone. Otherwise play is continuous.

Scoring: Attacking team gets 1 point for a pass received and controlled in the opponent's end zone. Team scoring the most points wins.

Practice Tips: Use smaller end zones to make it more difficult to score points and larger end zones to make it more difficult for defending players to prevent scores. Restrictions on players also increase difficulty. For example, to discourage excessive dribbling, limit players to three or fewer touches of the ball before passing.

34

Pass and Receive to Score

Minutes: 20-25   **Players:**   Two equal teams of 4-7

Objectives: Improve passing and receiving skills; improve one-on-one marking; develop endurance

Setup: Using markers, outline an area about 40 by 40 yards. Use cones or flags to represent five small goals 2 to 3 yards wide randomly positioned within the area. Colored scrimmage vests differentiate teams. One team has the ball. Do not use goalkeepers.

Procedure: Begin with a kickoff from the center of the area. Teams can score in all five goals and must defend all five goals. Players attempt to pass the ball through a goal to a teammate. The ball may be passed through either side of a goal, but not twice consecutively through the same goal. Play is continuous. Change of possession does not occur after each goal. Other than the method of scoring, regular soccer rules apply.

Scoring: Team gets 1 point each time a player completes a pass through a goal to a teammate. Team scoring the most points wins.

Practice Tips: Prohibiting consecutive scores through the same goal encourages players to constantly switch the point of attack to attack the goal area with the fewest opponents. Require one-on-one marking to reduce the space and time available for players to pass and receive the ball.

35

Soccer Volleyball

Minutes: 30   **Players:** Two equal teams of 3-6

Objectives: Improve ability to pass and receive bouncing balls and balls dropping out of the air

Setup: Play on a volleyball court if available. If not, using markers, outline a rectangular area about 20 by 40 yards. Stretch a net or rope about 6 feet high across the center of the court. Station one team on each side of the net. One soccer ball is required.

Procedure: Players use only heads or feet to play the ball. Flip a coin to decide which team serves first. The server positions with the ball behind the end line. The ball must be chipped over the net and land within the opponents' court to constitute a good serve. The ball may bounce once before it is returned, but it may be returned with a first-time volley. (This applies to all plays, not only service returns.) Teammates are also permitted to pass to one another in the air before returning the ball over the net. A fault occurs when

- the serve or return fails to clear the net,
- the serve or return lands out-of-bounds,
- the ball is allowed to bounce more than once, or
- a player uses his or her arms or hands to pass or control the ball.

If the serving team commits a fault they lose serve to opponents.

Scoring: Only serving team can score. Serving team gets 1 point for each fault by receiving team. The first team to score 21 points wins. Play three games.

Practice Tips: Soccer volleyball is a good choice for the day after a match when players may be sore and their muscles tired.

Dribbling, Shielding, and Tackling Skills

36

Shadow Dribble

Minutes: 10   **Players:**   Unlimited (in pairs)

Objectives: Improve dribbling skills through the development of body feints, quick changes of speed and direction, and deceptive foot movements

Setup: Pair each player with a teammate. Using markers, outline a rectangular area about 50 by 60 yards; if a regulation field is available play on one half of the field. Each player has a ball.

Procedure: Players dribble randomly throughout the area, one partner leading and the other closely following. The trailing player tries to imitate, or shadow, the dribbling movements of the leader. Players change positions every 45-60 seconds, the leader becoming the follower. The coach keeps time.

Scoring: None

Practice Tips: Dribblers should keep their heads up as much as possible to ensure good field vision. Emphasize fluid, controlled movement with the ball. Make exercise more challenging by requiring players to increase their dribbling speed.

37

Soccer Marbles

Minutes: 6-12   **Players:** Unlimited (groups of 3)

Objectives: Improve dribbling and shielding skills

Setup: Using markers, outline a rectangular area approximately 20 by 30 yards for each group. Position players, each with a ball, on the perimeter of the area. Designate one player as "it."

Procedure: The player who is "it" dribbles into the area. The others closely follow and attempt to pass and hit the dribbler's ball with their own. The "it" player protects his or her ball by dribbling randomly within the area, making quick changes of speed and direction while shielding the ball with his or her body. Players take turns being "it" for 2 minutes each.

Scoring: Assess the player who is "it" 1 penalty point each time his or her ball is contacted by one of the other balls. Player receiving fewest penalty points wins.

Practice Tips: Add an additional chaser to the game or reduce the size of the area to make the game more challenging for advanced players.

38

Speed Dribbling

Minutes: 10   **Players:** Unlimited (in pairs)

Objectives: Improve dribbling speed and endurance

Setup: Use one sideline of a regulation field as the starting line and the opposite sideline as the halfway line. If a regulation field is not available, place markers to designate starting and halfway lines about 60 yards apart. All players, each with a ball, position an equal distance apart on the starting line.

Procedure: On the coach's command "Go," one member of each pair dribbles to the halfway line at top speed, turns, dribbles back to the starting line, and tags his or her partner who immediately dribbles the circuit at top speed. Run a minimum of five races with a short rest period between.

Scoring: The pair dribbling both balls to the starting line first wins the race.

Practice Tips: The technique used for dribbling at speed differs from that used when dribbling for close control. Players should push the ball 2 or 3 yards ahead and use longer strides rather than keep the ball close to their feet. Adjust the race distance to the ages and abilities of the players. Shorten the distance to the halfway line to 30 to 40 yards for players 10 years and under.

39

Slalom Dribbling Races

Minutes: 10-15   **Players:**   Three or more equal teams of 3-5

Objectives: Improve dribbling speed and control and improve fitness

Setup: Position each team in single file on a starting line facing 6 to 8 markers set out in a straight line. Allow 3 to 4 yards between markers. The first player in each line has a ball.

Procedure: On the coach's command "Go," the first player in each line dribbles as fast as possible through the slalom course, weaving in and out of the markers front to back to front. Upon return to the starting line the dribbler gives the ball to the next player in line. All players dribble the course in turn. The team whose players complete the course first wins. Repeat at least five times with a short rest period between each race.

Scoring: Teams get 10 points for winning, 8 points for second place, and 6 points for third place. Penalize players 1 point for each marker bypassed or knocked over. Determine team point totals by subtracting the total number of penalty points from points awarded for the team's order of finish in the race. The first team to score 50 points wins.

Practice Tips: Reduce the space between markers, increase the number of markers, or do both to require more precise ball control of advanced players.

40

Takeovers

Minutes: 5-10   **Players:** Unlimited

Objectives: Develop ability to exchange possession (take over the ball) from a dribbling teammate

Setup: Using markers, outline a rectangular area 25 by 30 yards. Station all players within the area, with one ball for each 2 players.

Procedure: All players begin to move randomly throughout the playing area. Those with a ball dribble, those without a ball jog at half-speed. On the coach's command, dribblers exchange possession of the ball with one of the free players, using the ''takeover'' technique. Takeover commands should be issued every 10 to 15 seconds.

Scoring: None

Practice Tips: A dribbler should control the ball with the foot farthest from an imaginary defender as he or she prepares to exchange possession with a teammate. Players about to execute a takeover should communicate with each other through verbal signals or subtle body movements.

41

Cone-to-Cone

Minutes: 12-18 (periods of 60 seconds each)

Players: Unlimited (in pairs)

Objectives: Develop deceptive dribbling movements and body feints to unbalance an opponent; improve mobility and fitness

Setup: Each pair uses a portion of the sideline or end line of the field. Place two cones 10 yards apart on the line. Partners station on opposite sides of the line facing one another. One player (attacker) has the ball.

Procedure: The attacker attempts to dribble laterally to either cone before the defender can position there. The defender may not steal the ball and neither player may cross the line that separates them. Players switch roles for the second period.

Scoring: Attacker gets 1 point each time he or she beats the defender to a cone. The player scoring the most points in two periods wins. Play six games.

Practice Tips: The dribbler should combine feinting movements with quick changes of speed and direction to unbalance the defender. Increase the distance between cones to make the game more physically demanding. Play several games or organize a tournament with winners advancing against a different opponent.

42

Zonal Dribbling

Minutes: 10-15   **Players:**   Unlimited (groups of 4)

Objectives: Improve dribbling skills; develop tackling skills

Setup: Using markers, outline a 10- by 40-yard area for each group, divided into four zones 10 by 10 yards. Position one player in each zone. The player in Zone #1 faces the others and has the ball.

Procedure: The player in Zone 1 attempts to dribble past the players defending Zones 2, 3, and 4. Defenders are restricted to their assigned zone and must use the block or the poke tackle to steal the ball. If the dribbler beats a defender he or she continues forward to take on the player in the next zone. A defender who steals the ball immediately returns it to the dribbler, so he or she can advance to take on the defender in the next zone. After reaching the last zone the dribbler remains there to play as a defender for the next round. Each of the original defenders moves forward one zone. The player who moves into Zone 1 becomes the dribbler for Round 2. Repeat until all players have taken five turns as the dribbler.

Scoring: Dribbler gets 1 point for each defender beaten. The player with the most points after five turns as the dribbler wins.

Practice Tips: To begin play station defenders on the back line of their zone. From this position they can move forward to challenge once the dribbler enters their area. Prohibit defenders from using slide tackles.

43

Wolves and Sheep

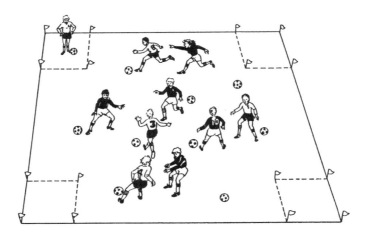

Minutes: 10-15   **Players:**   Unlimited (two equal teams)

Objectives: Improve dribbling speed and control

Setup: Using markers, outline a rectangular area 35 by 40 yards. Designate a safety zone 5 by 5 yards in each corner of the area. Assign a name to each team; for example, "Blues" and "Reds." Colored scrimmage vests differentiate teams. All players, each with a ball, station within the area.

Procedure: All players dribble randomly—but not in the safety zones—maintaining close control of the ball. After 30 to 45 seconds the coach shouts one of the team names, for example, "Blues!" All Blue team players immediately try to dribble into a safety zone. "Red" players leave their balls and attempt to tag (with the hand) Blue players before the Blues can reach a safety zone. The players who chase are referred to as "Wolves" while those trying to flee ino a safety zone are "Sheep." Sheep may not be tagged once they enter a safety zone. After each round all players return to the center of the area and begin dribbling to restart play. Repeat several times, with teams alternating as Wolves and Sheep.

Scoring: Each sheep who reaches a safety zone before being tagged gets 1 team point. The team scoring the most points after several repetitions of the game wins.

Practice Tips: Encourage Sheep to use quick changes of speed and direction to avoid being tagged. For advanced players enlarge the playing area, and require Wolves to dribble a ball while giving chase.

44

Tackle One and All

Minutes: 10-15   **Players:**   10-15

Objectives: Develop the block tackle; improve dribbling and shielding skills; improve fitness

Setup: Using markers, outline a rectangular area about 30 by 35 yards. Designate 2 players as defenders, who position without balls outside the area. All other players, each with a ball, station within the area.

Procedure: Players begin dribbling randomly within the area. On command the defenders enter the area and attempt to tackle a dribbler and gain possession of a ball. Dribblers should use shielding skills coupled with sudden changes of speed and direction to avoid the defenders. A dribbler who loses possession of the ball becomes a defender and must try to steal someone else's ball. A defender gaining possession of a ball becomes a dribbler.

Scoring: None

Practice Tips: Require defenders to use the block tackle when attempting to steal a ball. Prohibit use of the slide tackle because of the crowded conditions and the increased likelihood of injury. Use three or more defenders to make the game more challenging for the dribblers.

45

All vs. All

Minutes: 10-15   **Players:** 10-20

Objectives: Improve dribbling, shielding, and tackling skills; improve fitness

Setup: Using markers, outline a rectangular area about 20 by 30 yards. All players, each with a ball, station within the playing area.

Procedure: Players begin by dribbling among themselves randomly. On a signal from the coach it becomes "All vs. All." Each player attempts to steal balls from other players and kick them out of the area while protecting his or her own ball. A player whose ball is kicked out of the area is eliminated. The game continues until only one player remains in possession of his or her ball. Repeat the game several times.

Scoring: None

Practice Tips: Vary the size of the area depending upon the number of players. The space should be crowded so that players must execute dribbling and feinting skills in close proximity to teammates. Players should use either the block or the poke tackle when attempting to steal a teammate's ball. Prohibit use of the slide tackle because of the crowded conditions. Players who are eliminated should retrieve their ball and practice ball juggling outside of the playing area until the next game.

46

Touch-and-Go Dribbling

Minutes: 15   **Players:**   Two teams of 5-8

Objectives: Improve dribbling skills

Setup: Using markers, outline a rectangular area about 40 by 25 yards, divided by a midline. Station a team in each half. Position one player from each team, the "chaser," in the opponents' half of the field. All players have a ball.

Procedure: The "chaser" tries to tag as many opponents as possible with his or her hand while dribbling his or her ball. The "chaser" may not tag the same opponent twice in succession. Opponents avoid the "chaser" by using quick changes of speed and direction while dribbling. Every 3 minutes stop the game momentarily and select different players as "chasers."

Scoring: Team gets 1 point for each opponent tagged by a chaser. Teams keep a running total of their points. Team scoring the most points wins.

Practice Tips: Vary the area acording to the number of players involved.

47

Too Few Balls, Too Many Players

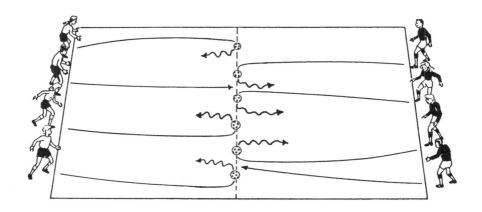

Minutes: 10-15   **Players:**   Two equal teams of 4-8

Objectives: Improve dribbling speed and develop endurance

Setup: Using markers, outline a rectangular area 25 by 50 yards, divided by a midline. Station teams on opposite end lines with players an equal distance apart, facing the center of the field. Place balls along the midline (two fewer balls than the total number of players involved). Colored scrimmage vests differentiate teams.

Procedure: On the command "Go," players from both teams sprint to the midline, compete for possession of a ball, and attempt to return it over their own end line by dribbling. Since there are two fewer balls than players, the players who do not immediately secure a ball try to steal a ball from one of their opponents and return it over their own team's end line. The round ends when all balls have been returned over an end line. Replace all balls on the midline and repeat the round. Play at least 10 rounds.

Scoring: Team gets 1 point for each ball returned over its end line. A ball must be dribbled under control over an end line to score a point. The team scoring the most points wins.

Practice Tips: As a safety precaution prohibit slide tackles.

48

Dribble the Maze and Score

Minutes: 10-15   **Players:**   4-6 (3-5 shooters; 1 goalkeeper)

Objectives: Improve shooting skills; develop dribbling skills; provide pressure training for the goalkeeper

Setup: Using markers, outline a rectangular area 30 by 40 yards, divided by a midline. Position a regulation goal at one end of the area. Station shooters, each with a ball, at the opposite end. Place pairs of cones or flags to represent five small goals organized in a zigzag pattern in the half of the area occupied by the shooters.

Procedure: Each shooter in turn dribbles through all five small goals before pushing the ball into the goalkeeper's half of the field and shooting to score. As soon as the shot is taken, the next shooter in line begins his or her dribble through the small goals. Shooters should quickly retrieve their ball after each shot and return to the starting position. Continue until each player has attempted 20 shots at goal. Goalkeeper attempts to save all shots.

Scoring: A shooter gets 2 points for a goal scored, 1 point for a shot on goal saved by the goalkeeper. Player who totals the most points wins.

Practice Tips: Position the small goals so that shooters are required to change direction and maintain close control of the ball when dribbling through them. This game also provides excellent shot-saving practice for goalkeepers. Two goalkeepers can be used in this drill, one saving while the other rests.

49

Breakaway and Score

Minutes: 10-15   **Players:**   Two teams of 5-8

Objectives: Improve dribbling speed and develop endurance

Setup: Play on a regulation field with goals. All players, each with a ball, station in the center circle. Name each team; for example, "Strikers" and "Kickers." Colored scrimmage vests differentiate teams. There are no goal-keepers.

Procedure: Each team defends a goal and can score in the opponents' goal. To begin all players dribble in the center circle. After 30 to 40 seconds the coach shouts a team name; for example, Strikers. At that signal the Strikers leave the circle to dribble at top speed toward the Kickers' goal. The Kickers leave their balls to give chase, trying to catch the dribblers and steal their balls before they can shoot to score. All shots must be taken from within the penalty area. A defender who steals a ball must dribble it back into the center circle. Repeat the game at least six times, teams alternating as attackers and defenders.

Scoring: Attacking team gets 1 point for each goal; defending team gets 1 point for each ball stolen and dribbled back to the center circle; team scoring the most points wins.

Practice Tips: Adjust the field to the age and abilities of players; for younger players use a three-quarter-length field. Require defending players to recover to a position goalside of their opponent before challenging their opponent for the ball. Prohibit slide tackles or tackles initiated from behind the dribbler.

Heading Skills

50

Heading Races

Minutes: 5-10   **Players:**   Two equal teams of 5-8

Objectives: Develop proper heading technique

Setup: Position teams side by side in single file with at least 2 yards between teams. Station 1 player as server about 2 yards in front of each team, facing the first player in line. Each team has one ball.

Procedure: On the command "Go," servers toss a ball to the first player in their line, who heads it back to the server and then drops to his or her knees. Servers immediately toss to the next player in line who also heads and then kneels. Servers continue through the team until all players have headed and are kneeling. The team whose players are all kneeling first wins. Players then stand and rotate positions in preparation for the next race. The original server moves to the back of the line, the first player in line becomes the server, and everyone else moves one spot forward. Take only a brief pause between races.

Scoring: First team to win six races wins the series.

Practice Tips: Proper technique is required to generate power and accuracy to the headed ball. Players should arch the upper trunk backward and then snap forward as the ball arrives. They should contact the ball on the flat surface of the forehead and attempt to head it directly into the server's hands.

51

Triangular Heading Game

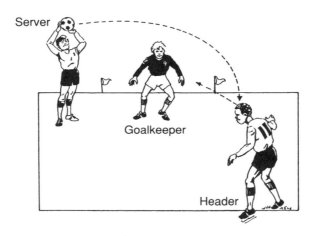

Server

Goalkeeper

Header

Minutes: 10-15 **Players:** Unlimited (groups of 3)

Objectives: Develop the heading skills used to score goals

Setup: Using markers, outline an area 10 by 10 yards for each group. Place flags or cones to represent a goal 4 yards wide on one side of the area. Position one player as a goalkeeper, one player as a server to the side of the goal, and one player as the "header" 8 yards front and center of the goal. Each group has a ball.

Procedure: The server tosses the ball upward so it will drop near the center of the area. The "header" judges the flight of the ball, moves toward it, and tries to score by heading past the goalkeeper. Players rotate positions after each header and repeat.

Scoring: Give 1 point for each header scored. The player scoring the most points wins.

Practice Tips: Players should head the ball on a downward plane toward a corner of the goal when attempting to score. Allow beginning players to head the ball with both feet on the ground; require advanced players to jump and head the ball.

52

Jump Header Competition

Minutes: 10   **Players:**   Unlimited (groups of 3)

Objectives: Improve jump header technique and timing; develop leg strength and muscular endurance

Setup: Station each group within a rectangular area 5 by 10 yards. Position a server at each end with a ball. The third player positions in the middle of the area facing one of the servers.

Procedure: Servers take turns tossing a ball toward the central player (header) who jumps and heads each toss back to the server from whom it came. After heading 30 tosses the header exchanges places with one of the servers. Repeat the exercise until each player has taken two turns as the header.

Scoring: Players compete within their group. The header gets 1 point for each ball returned so that the server can catch it directly out of the air. The player scoring the most points wins.

Practice Tips: Encourage players to jump vertically, arch the upper trunk backward, and then snap forward to contact the ball on their forehead. For younger players decrease the total number of balls headed (perhaps 10 to 12 headers per round). The head should be firmly positioned with eyes open and mouth closed at moment of contact with ball.

53

Heading Goal-to-Goal

Minutes: 15   **Players:** Unlimited (in pairs)

Objectives: Improve heading technique

Setup: Using markers, outline a rectangular area 10 by 12 yards for each pair. Position cones or flags to mark a goal 4 yards wide at each end of the area. Position a player in each goal. One player (the server) has the ball.

Procedure: The server tosses the ball upward so that it will drop near the center of the area. The other player moves forward from his or her goal and tries to score by heading the ball past the server into the goal. After each attempt players return to their respective goals. Repeat 50 times with players alternating turns serving and heading.

Scoring: Players compete with their partner. Give 1 point for each goal scored. The player scoring the most points wins.

Practice Tips: Encourage players to jump vertically, arch their upper body back at the waist, and then snap forward to contact the ball on the flat surface of the forehead. The head should be firmly positioned with eyes open and mouth closed at moment of contact with ball.

54

Diving Headers Game

Minutes: 10-15 (or predetermined number of points)

Players: Two equal teams of 4-6; 3 neutrals

Objectives: Develop the ability to score from dive headers

Setup: Teams position side by side in single file facing a regulation goal at a distance of about 15 yards. If a regulation field is marked, have the teams line up at the top of the penalty area. Designate 2 neutral servers and a neutral goalkeeper from players not on a team. Position a server 6 yards to each side of the goal with a supply of balls.

Procedure: Servers take turns tossing balls into the area front and center of the goal. The tosses should be parallel to the ground at a height of 3 to 4 feet. Players from each team take turns moving forward and then diving to head the ball on goal. The goalkeeper tries to save all shots.

Scoring: Give 2 points for each goal scored and 1 point for a ball headed on goal but saved by the goalkeeper. Team scoring the most points wins.

Practice Tips: Diving headers are especially fun to practice on a wet, soggy field. Correct technique is, however, very important. Players should dive forward parallel to the ground and contact the ball on the forehead. Arms and hands are extended downward to cushion the impact with the ground. This game is not appropriate for very young players who lack adequate strength and coordination.

55

Score by Headers Only (With Neutrals)

Minutes: 15   **Players:** 12 (two teams of 4 plus 4 neutrals)

Objectives: Improve ability to score from headers; develop endurance

Setup: Using markers, outline a rectangular area 40 by 50 yards. Use markers to represent a goal 4 yards wide at the center of each end line. Colored scrimmage vests differentiate teams. One ball is used.

Procedure: Coach tosses the ball upward in the center of the field. Player who jumps highest to catch it gets possession. Each team defends a goal and attempts to score in the opponent's goal. Players pass by throwing and catching, not kicking, the ball. Goals are scored when a ball tossed by a teammate is headed through the opponents' goal. Players may take up to five steps with the ball before passing to a teammate. Players violating the five-step rule lose possession to the opposing team. The four neutrals play with the team in possession to create an 8 vs. 4-player advantage. There are no goalkeepers, but players may intercept passes or block shots with their hands.

Defending team gains possession of the ball when they intercept an opponent's pass, when an opponent drops the ball to the ground, when an opponent takes more than five steps with the ball, or when the ball is played out of bounds by an opponent. Defenders must not wrestle the ball from an opponent.

Scoring: Team scoring the most goals wins.

Practice Tips: Emphasize short, accurate passes rather than long tosses with high risk of interception. Head the ball downward toward the goal line when attempting to score.

Shooting Skills

56

Instep Shooting

Minutes: 15-20   **Players:**   Unlimited (groups of 3)

Objectives: Develop shooting power and accuracy

Setup: Use cones or flags to represent a regulation size goal for each group. Position two shooters 30 yards front and center of the goal with a supply of balls. The third player positions in the goal as a neutral goalkeeper.

Procedure: Shooters take turns attempting to score from a distance of 20 yards or greater. Shooters start at a distance of 30 yards, dribble several yards towards goal, and then shoot to score, using the instep drive technique. The goalkeeper tries to save all shots.

Scoring: Shooter gets 2 points for a goal scored and 1 point for a shot on goal saved by the goalkeeper. Shooter receives 1 penalty point for a shot that travels to the side of or over the goal. The first player to score 20 points wins the round. Play three rounds.

Practice Tips: Players rotate after each round so that each takes a turn as the goalkeeper. To make the game more challenging require advanced players to swerve their shots by striking the ball with either the inside or outside portion of the instep. Adjust the shooting distance to the age and abilities of players. Reduce the distance to 12 yards or less for players 12 years and under.

57

First-Time Shooting Competition

Pass/shot ----→
Run ———→

Minutes: 15

Players: Unlimited (equal teams of 4-6 players plus 1 neutral)

Objectives: Develop ability to shoot first time with power and accuracy

Setup: Position teams side by side in single file about 35 yards from goal. Each player has a ball. Position 1 player as a "target" about 20 yards from goal, facing each team. Position a neutral goalkeeper in goal.

Procedure: The first shooter in Line 1 passes to his or her team's target, who pushes the ball about a yard to either side. The shooter immediately runs forward and shoots first time from a distance of 18 yards or greater. The goalkeeper tries to save all shots. The shooter should follow up the shot and may score off a rebound if the goalkeeper fails to hold the ball. Once the keeper has the ball, however, or if the shot travels wide or over the goal, the first shooter in Line 2 passes to his or her team's target and shoots to score. Play is continuous as players from the two teams alternate turns.

Scoring: Team gets 1 point for a shot on goal that the goalkeeper saves and 2 points for a goal scored. Team scoring the most points wins.

Practice Tips: Designate one player on each team to keep score. The instep drive is the preferred shooting technique. Shots should be aimed low and to the side of the goalkeeper. Reduce the shooting distance for younger players.

58

Pressure Shooting Competition

Minutes: 20   **Players:**   Unlimited (groups of 3)

Objectives: Develop shooting skills under simulated match pressures; improve fitness

Setup: Play on one end of a regulation field with a goal positioned on the end line. Position one player as a shooter, one as a server, and one as a goalkeeper. Station the shooter 20 to 25 yards from the end line, back to the goal. The server faces the shooter from a distance of 5 yards with a supply of 8 to 10 balls.

Procedure: The server tosses a ball past the shooter who quickly turns, sprints to the ball, and shoots to score. The shooter must strike the ball first time, then quickly return to the starting position. The server then tosses another ball past the shooter. Continue until the supply of balls is used up. The goalkeeper tries to save all shots. Players rotate positions after each round. Play two rounds of shooting for each player.

Scoring: Shooter gets 1 point for a shot on goal and 2 points for a goal scored. The player who totals the most points wins.

Practice Tips: This game provides excellent training for strikers and attacking midfielders. Require first-time shooting; require players to alternate shooting with left and right feet. Reduce the shooting distance to 12 to 15 yards for younger players.

59

Serve and Shoot

Minutes: 2-3 per round   **Players:** 7

Objectives: Develop ability to shoot with power and accuracy; provide goalkeeper shot-stopping practice

Setup: Position a cone on the penalty arc front and center of a regulation goal. Position 5 servers, each with a supply of balls, around the perimeter of the penalty area. Station the shooter next to the marker on the penalty arc. The goalkeeper positions in goal.

Procedure: Each server, in turn, passes a ball into the penalty area. The shooter moves quickly to the ball, controls it with his or her first touch, and then shoots to score with the second touch. The goalkeeper attempts to save all shots. After each shot the shooter must run back around the cone before receiving the next serve. The shooter takes 10 shots and then switches positions with one of the servers. Continue the game until all players have taken two turns as the shooter.

Scoring: Players get 1 point for a shot on goal and 2 points for a goal scored. Player scoring the most points wins.

Practice Tips: Servers should vary the type of serve (rolling, bouncing, lofted balls). Require first-time (one-touch) shooting to make the game more challenging.

60

Shooting Fish in a Barrel

Minutes: 15-20   **Players:**   Two teams of 3-5

Objectives: Develop instep shooting technique; practice attacking and defending in small groups

Setup: Evenly distribute 12 to 18 cones within the center circle of the field. Station both teams outside the circle. Give one team possession of the ball, at least 15 yards from the circle. Opposing team positions between the ball and the circle.

Procedure: Goals are scored by shooting a ball into the circle and knocking down one or more cones. The team with the ball attacks while the other defends. Teams immediately switch roles upon change of possession. All shots must be taken with the instep of the foot from outside the circle. A ball traveling completely through the circle is "live" and can be played by the team that retrieves it first. A ball that stops within the circle is "dead;" the team that played the ball into the circle loses possession. A player from the opposing team retrieves the ball and initiates the attack from at least 15 yards outside the circle. Players are not permitted to enter the circle except to retrieve a stopped ball. Continue the game until all cones have been knocked down.

Scoring: Team gets 1 point for each cone knocked down. The team scoring the most points wins. Play five games.

Practice Tips: As a variation increase the number of players per team and use two balls.

61

Shooting Cones in the Safety Zones

Minutes: 15 (or until all cones are knocked over)

Players: Two equal teams of 4-7

Objectives: Improve shooting and passing accuracy; develop the group tactics used in attack and defense; develop endurance

Setup: Using markers, outline a rectangular area 30 by 40 yards, with a safety zone 5 yards wide at each end. Place 8 to 12 cones within an area 5 by 10 feet in the center of each safety zone. Colored scrimmage vests differentiate teams. One team has the ball.

Procedure: Players try to knock over opponents' cones by shooting or passing the ball from outside the safety zones. Change of possession occurs when an opponent steals the ball, when the ball travels out of play, when a cone is knocked over, or when the ball passes through a safety zone and out of the field area. Otherwise, basic soccer rules apply. Players are not permitted to enter either safety zone except to retrieve a ball. Cones knocked over remain down to indicate the score at any point in the game.

Scoring: Team gets 1 point for each cone knocked over. Team scoring the most points wins.

Practice Tips: Adjust the size of the area to the number and ages of players. As a variation increase the number of players per team and have two or three balls in play at the same time.

62

Shoot to Score

Minutes: 15-20 **Players:** 6 (2 teams of 2 plus 2 neutrals)

Objectives: Develop shooting skills; improve fitness; provide goalkeeper training

Setup: Position both teams in a penalty area of a regulation field. Station the server (neutral) at the top (front) of the penalty area with a dozen balls. Colored scrimmage vests differentiate teams. The goalkeeper (neutral) protects the common goal.

Procedure: The server tosses a ball into the penalty area, where both teams vie for possession. The team gaining possession attempts to score while their opponents defend. Teams immediately switch roles upon loss of possession. The keeper tries to save all shots. Stop play momentarily after a goal is scored, when the keeper makes a save, or when the ball is kicked out of bounds. The server immediately restarts play by tossing another ball into the area. Continue the competition until the supply of balls is used up. Repeat the round after a short rest.

Scoring: Team scoring the most goals wins the round. Play 5 rounds.

Practice Tips: Emphasize shooting accuracy as well as power. Encourage players to release their shots at any opportunity. They must learn to create goals out of half chances.

63

Game With a Central Goal

Minutes: 15-20   **Players:** Two equal teams of 3-5 plus 1 neutral

Objectives: Develop shooting skills; provide shot-stopping practice for goalkeeper; improve fitness

Setup: Using markers, outline an area about 40 by 40 yards. Place two cones or flags in the center of the area to represent a goal 8 yards wide. Position a goalkeeper (neutral) in goal. Colored scrimmage vests differentiate teams. One team has a ball.

Procedure: Teams can score through either side of the central goal. The goalkeeper must constantly readjust his or her position in response to the movement of the ball. The keeper attempts to save all shots. After each save the goalkeeper tosses the ball to a corner of the playing area, where teams compete for possession. Change of possession occurs after a goal is scored, when the ball travels out of the field area, or when a defending player steals the ball. A ball played out-of-bounds is returned by a throw-in. Otherwise, play is continuous as teams switch from attack to defense and vice versa upon change of possession.

Scoring: A shot that passes between the cones (or flags) below the height of the goalkeeper's head counts as a goal scored. Team scoring the most goals wins.

Practice Tips: Require defending team to use a one-on-one marking scheme to reduce time and space available to attacking players.

64

Long-Distance Shooting Game

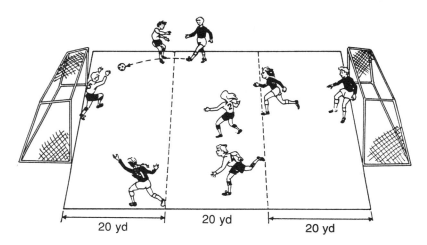

20 yd	20 yd	20 yd

Minutes: 15-20   **Players:** Two teams of 4

Objectives: Develop ability to shoot with power and accuracy from outside the penalty area; develop endurance; provide goalkeeper training

Setup: Using markers, outline a rectangular area 40 by 60 yards. Divide the field lengthwise into three equal zones. Position a regulation goal at the center of each end line. One team has a ball. One player on each team is goalkeeper.

Procedure: Begin with a kickoff from the center of the field. Teams defend a goal and try to score in the opponent's goal. Regular soccer rules apply, except that all shots must be taken from 20 yards or more.

Scoring: Team gets 2 points for a goal scored and 1 point for a shot on goal saved by the goalkeeper. Team scoring the most points wins.

Practice Tips: Encourage players to shoot at every opportunity. Adjust the area to the age and abilities of players. Require players under 12 years to take shots from a distance of 12 yards or greater.

65

Volley Shooting Game

Minutes: 20-25   **Players:** Two equal teams of 4-6

Objectives: Improve volley shooting skills and develop endurance

Setup: Using markers, outline a rectangular area 40 by 50 yards and position a regulation goal on the center of each end line. Colored scrimmage vests differentiate teams. One team has a ball. There are no goalkeepers.

Procedure: Each team defends a goal and can score in the opponent's goal. Interpassing among teammates is accomplished by throwing and catching, not kicking, the ball. A player may take no more than five steps with the ball before passing to a teammate. Change of possession occurs when a defending player intercepts a pass, the ball goes out of play, the ball is dropped to the ground, a player takes too many steps with the ball, or a goal is scored. Players score by volley shooting a teammate's pass out of the air through opponents' goal.

Scoring: Team that scores the most goals wins.

Practice Tips: Encourage players to use short accurate passes rather than long tosses with little chance of completion. As volley shooting is a difficult skill to execute successfully, this game may not be appropriate for beginning players.

Part III

GAMES FOR TACTICAL TRAINING

Soccer tactics involve decision making and problem solving. It is essential that players understand the tactical concepts upon which their actions are based. Decisions such as how and when to pass, where to position oneself in relation to the ball and opponents, and whether to shoot or dribble in a specific situation are just a few examples of the many choices that confront players during the course of a match. The ability to make correct judgments under the pressures of match competition is just as important as the ability to perform the skills used in those situations. Players who make the right decisions generally experience the greatest success.

Tactics are applied at three levels—individual, group, and team. Individual tactics encompass the principles of attack and defense used in a one-on-one situation. Group tactics involve 3 or more players in combination (2 vs. 1, 2 vs. 2, 3 vs. 2, etc). Tactics may also be applied by the team as a whole. The ultimate objective of team tactics is to make the whole team greater than the sum of its parts (players).

Tactical training should start with the most basic tactical unit (1 vs. 1), gradually progress to group tactics, and finally to team tactics. It is important to remember, however, that tactics are of little or no use if players cannot execute basic soccer skills. For this reason the teaching of tactics should not be emphasized until players have mastered basic soccer skills.

The games described in this part are arranged in a progressive sequence, beginning with individual tactics and progressing through group situations. All games can be adapted to the age, abilities, and developmental level of the players. By altering factors such as the size of playing area, the number of players, the types of passes required, or the speed of repetition, games can be made either more or less challenging to players.

Individual and Team
Tactics

66

1 vs. 1

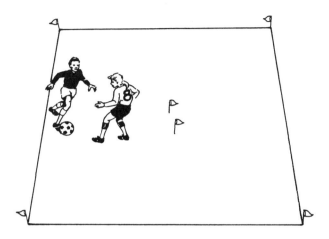

Minutes: 1 each game (minimum of 5)   **Players:** Unlimited (in pairs)

Objectives: Develop the attacking and defending tactics used in a one-on-one situation; improve dribbling, tackling, and shielding skills; develop fitness

Setup: Using markers, outline a square area 15 by 15 yards. Place a pair of cones or flags to represent a common goal 1 yard wide in the center of the area. Divide players into pairs, each with a ball. One player in each pair has possession of the ball.

Procedure: Each pair plays one-on-one within the area. Players score by dribbling past their opponent and passing through the goal. Goals can be scored through either side of the central goal. Change of possession occurs when the defending player steals the ball or when the ball travels out of the area. Players immediately change roles with each loss of possession. Play a series of 1-minute games with a rest of 30 to 60 seconds between games.

Scoring: The player scoring the most goals wins.

Practice Tips: Encourage players to make an immediate transition from defense to attack and vice versa upon loss of possession. Increase the size of the goal and shorten the game to 30 seconds for players under 10 years.

67

Individual Attack and Defense

Minutes: 15   **Players:** Unlimited (in pairs)

Objectives: Develop players' ability to attack and defend in one-on-one situations

Setup: Group players into pairs. Using markers, outline a rectangular area 10 by 25 yards for each pair. Station one player from each pair at each end of the field. Place two markers 4 yards apart on one end line to represent a goal. Each pair has a ball; the player nearer the goal has possession.

Procedure: The player with the ball serves a lofted pass to his or her partner and immediately moves forward off the goal line to play as a defender. The player receiving the ball attempts to beat the defender by dribbling past him or her through the goal. After the attacker has dribbled through the goal, or the defender has gained possession of the ball, players switch positions and repeat.

Scoring: Attacker gets 1 point for dribbling past the defender and through the goal. Player scoring the most points wins.

Practice Tips: Encourage the defender to slow his or her approach when nearing the attacker and assume a proper defensive posture. The attacker should take-on (dribble past) the defender at speed. Reduce the length of the area for younger players.

68

1 vs. 1 With Support

Minutes: 12-16 (6-8 2-minute rounds)   **Players:**   Two teams of 2

Objectives: Develop individual attacking and defending tactics and improve fitness

Setup: Using markers, outline a rectangular area 10 by 20 yards. One player on each team positions as a goal by standing with feet spread apart on his or her respective end line. The remaining 2 players station in the center of the area for one-on-one competition. One player has the ball.

Procedure: The player with the ball tries to score by dribbling past his or her opponent and passing the ball through the legs of the player positioned as a goal. If the defending player steals the ball he or she immediately attacks and tries to score through the opponents' goal. Players positioned as goals must remain stationary and may not stop the ball from rolling through their legs. Change of possession occurs if the defender steals the ball, if the ball travels out of play, and after each score. Play six to eight 2-minute rounds. Teammates switch positions after each round; the goalkeeper becomes the field player and vice versa. The coach keeps time.

Scoring: The team scoring the most goals after all rounds have been completed wins.

Practice Tips: The players positioned as "goals" should have an extra ball or two nearby. If the game ball is kicked out of the area the "goal" can immediately put another ball in play to prevent any stoppage in the action.

69

Playing the Wall (2 vs. 1)

Minutes: 15   **Players:** Unlimited (groups of 3)

Objectives: Develop ability to use the wall (give-and-go) pass to beat a defender; improve individual defending skills and tactics

Setup: Using markers, outline a square area 10 by 10 yards for each group. Designate 2 players as attackers and one as defender. Each group has a ball.

Procedure: Attackers use dribbling skills and passing combinations to keep the ball from the defender. A wall (give-and-go) pass occurs when an attacker passes to a nearby teammate and then sprints behind the defender to receive a return pass. If the defender steals the ball, he or she immediately returns it to the attackers, and the game continues. Play three 5-minute games, each player taking a turn as the defender.

Scoring: Attackers get 1 point for 5 consecutive passes and 2 points each time they beat the defender with a wall pass. Defender gets 2 points each time he or she wins possession of the ball or forces the attackers to play the ball outside the area. Player or players scoring the most points in 5 minutes wins the game.

Practice Tips: Successful execution of the wall pass requires timing and teamwork. The player with the ball commits the defender toward him or her; at the same time the supporting teammate positions with an open passing lane for the ball. Increase the area for beginning players to allow attackers more time to execute skills and make decisions.

70

Chip and Defend

Minutes: 10-15   **Players:**   Unlimited (groups of 3)

Objectives: Practice defending in a 2 vs. 1 situation; develop ability to chip (loft) passes; practice receiving and controlling lofted passes

Setup: Using markers, outline a rectangular area 15 by 30 yards for each group. Station one player (defender) with a ball near an end line. Station two players (attackers) at the opposite end of the area.

Procedure: The defender sends a lofted pass to the attackers and moves forward to challenge for possession. The attackers receive the ball and immediately advance to take on the defender in a 2 vs. 1 situation, aiming to dribble the ball over the end line. The attackers must stay within the area when attempting to beat the defender. Continue play until the defender steals the ball or the attackers advance the ball under control over the end line. Players then return to their original positions and repeat.

Scoring: Defender gets 1 point if he or she chips the ball so the attackers can receive it directly out of the air. Defender gets 1 additional point if he or she steals the ball from the attackers. Attackers get 1 point if they dribble over the end line. Play to 10 points, after which players rotate positions. Play three rounds, each player playing a turn as the defender.

Practice Tips: Players should have already developed the ability to send lofted passes over medium distances. Novices may not possess the skills or tactical knowledge required to play the game.

71

2 vs. 1 (Plus 1)

Minutes: 15-20   **Players:** Unlimited (teams of 2)

Objectives: Develop the ability to use the wall (give-and-go) pass to beat an opponent

Setup: Using markers, outline a rectangular area 15 by 25 yards and station two teams in it. Place cones or flags 4 yards apart at the center of each end line to represent goalposts. One team has a ball.

Procedure: Begin with a kickoff from the center of the field. Each team defends a goal and can score in the opponent's goal. One player on the defending team positions as the goalkeeper, the other as a single defender. Change of possession occurs when the defender steals the ball, the goalkeeper makes a save, the ball goes out of the playing area last touched by an attacker, or after a goal is scored. A defender who steals the ball must pass it back to the goalkeeper. Once the goalkeeper receives the ball, either from a teammate or after making a save, both players quickly move forward to attack the opponents' goal. One player on the team that lost possession immediately becomes goalkeeper, and the other plays as the single defender. Teammates take turns playing as the goalkeeper.

Scoring: Attackers get 1 point for each goal and 1 point each time they beat the defender with a wall (give-and-go) pass. Team scoring the most points wins.

Practice Tips: The attacking team should use the wall (give-and-go) pass to beat the defender whenever possible. Emphasize quick transitional play.

72

Pass and Support (3 vs. 1)

Minutes: 20 (four rounds of 5)   **Players:**   Unlimited (groups of 4)

Objectives: Develop the support movement used to create passing options for a player with the ball; improve passing and receiving skills

Setup: Using markers, outline a square area about 12 by 12 yards for each group. Designate 3 players as attackers and 1 as the defender. Each group has a ball.

Procedures: Attackers attempt to keep the ball from the defender by passing among themselves. If the defender steals the ball he or she immediately returns it to an attacker to continue the game. Play for 5 minutes, then designate a different player as the defender. Continue playing until all players have taken a turn as the defender.

Scoring: Attacking team gets 1 point for eight consecutive passes without loss of possession. Defender gets 1 point each time he or she steals the ball or causes the attackers to play the ball out of the area. Team scoring the most points after 5 minutes wins.

Practice Tips: Attacking players must continually adjust their positions to provide clear passing lanes for a teammate with the ball. Place restrictions on players to make the game more challenging. For example, limit attackers to a maximum of three touches to pass and receive the ball. For beginning players increase playing area and reduce the number of consecutive passes required to score a goal.

73

4-Corner Support Game

Minutes: 20-25 (5 rounds of 4-5) **Players:** 8

Objectives: Develop the passing combinations required to maintain possession of the ball

Setup: Using markers, outline a square area 25 by 25 yards. Place a cone at the midpoint of each of the four sides. Station a "support" player at each cone. Organize remaining players into teams of 2 and station both teams in the center of the area. One team has the ball. Scrimmage vests differentiate teams.

Procedure: The team with the ball tries to maintain possession. Support players join with the team in possession to create a 6 vs. 2 player advantage. Support players are restricted in their movements and must remain within 1 yard of either side of their cone. They are also limited to three touches to receive and pass the ball. Support players may receive the ball from, and pass it to, the central players only; they may not pass among themselves. Loss of possession occurs when a defending player steals the ball or when the ball goes out of play. Play for 4 to 5 minutes, after which central players switch position with the support players.

Scoring: Teams get 1 point for 8 consecutive passes. The team scoring the most points in 4 to 5 minutes wins.

Practice Tips: Impose restrictions to make the game more challenging for advanced players. For example, prohibit support players from passing the ball back to the same player who passed it to them. For young players reduce the area and award 1 point for 5 consecutive passes.

74

2 vs. 2 (Plus 3 in Support)

Minutes: 20

Players: 8 (two teams of 2, 3 support players, 1 target player)

Objectives: Improve ability to penetrate opposing defenses through combination passing and use of supporting teammates; practice defensive concepts of pressure and cover

Setup: Using markers, outline a rectangular area about 25 by 35 yards. Station two teams of 2 players each in the center of the area. Position 1 player at the center of each end line and each sideline. One team has the ball.

Procedure: Teams play 2 vs. 2 in the center of the area. Goals are scored by passing the ball to the "target" player positioned on the end line behind the defending team. The team with possession is allowed to pass the ball to the support players stationed on the sides and behind them to create a 5 vs. 2 attacking advantage. Support players must remain stationary; they must not move along the boundaries of the area to receive passes. Support players may, however, score goals. The defending team gains possession of the ball after a goal is scored, when the ball goes out of bounds off an attacking player, or when a defending player steals the ball. Upon change of possession the teams switch from attack to defense and vice versa. Play for 5 minutes, after which the support players switch positions with central players, form teams of 2 players each, and repeat the game. Continue until each team has played two 5-minute games in the center of the area.

Scoring: Attacking team gets 1 point for a pass completed to the "target" stationed on the end line behind the defending team. Team scoring the most points in 5 minutes wins.

Practice Tips: Place restrictions on advanced players to make the game more challenging. For example, limit support players to one- or two-touch passes or allow support players to move along the boundary lines.

75

3 vs. 2 (Plus 1)

Minutes: 15-20   **Players:** 6 (two teams of 3)

Objectives: Develop group tactics used in attack and defense and improve transition play

Setup: Using markers, outline a rectangular area 20 by 30 yards. Place 2 cones or flags 5 yards apart to represent goalposts at the center of each end line. One team has the ball.

Procedure: Begin with a kickoff from the center of the field. Each team defends a goal. The team with possession attacks with 3 players; opponents defend with 2 players and a goalkeeper. If a defending player steals the ball, he or she must pass it back to the goalkeeper before initiating an attack on the opponents' goal. The keeper then moves forward, joining teammates in the attack. One member of the team that lost possession immediately drops back to play as goalkeeper, while teammates position to defend the goal. Play is continuous as teams switch between attack and defense on change of possession. Teammates take turns playing in goal.

Scoring: Goals are scored by shooting the ball through the opponents' goal below the height of the goalkeeper's head. The team scoring the most goals wins.

Practice Tips: Stress quick transition from defense to attack on change of possession. Place extra balls behind each goal to avoid delays when a ball is shot past the goal. Adjust the area to the age and abilities of players, giving younger or less skilled players a larger area.

76

3 vs. 3 (Plus 1 Neutral)

Minutes: 15-20   **Players:** 7 (two teams of 3 plus 1 neutral)

Objectives: Develop the passing skills and group tactics used to maintain possession of the ball from opponents

Setup: Using markers, outline a square about 30 by 30 yards. Station both teams and the neutral player within the area. Colored scrimmage vests differentiate teams. One team has the ball.

Procedure: Each team tries to maintain possession of the ball. The neutral player always plays with the team in possession to create a 4 vs. 3 player advantage. Change of possession occurs when a defending player steals the ball, or when the ball goes out of play off a member of the attacking team.

Scoring: Team gets 1 point for six consecutive passes without loss of possession. The team scoring the most points wins.

Practice Tips: Limit the time and space available to advanced players by reducing the area. Increase the area and/or require fewer passes per goal scored for less skilled players.

77

Goal Kick and Recover Goalside

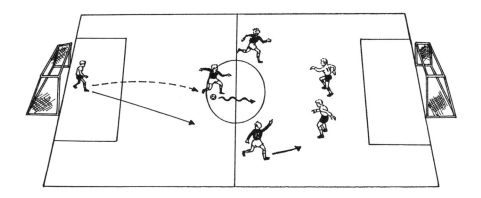

Minutes: 15   **Players:**   6 (two teams of 3)

Objectives: Develop distance and accuracy on goal kicks; improve endurance; practice defensive principle of delay/contain

Setup: Play on a regulation field with a regulation goal on each end line. There are no goalkeepers. One ball is required.

Procedure: Station players from one team in the center circle. Two opponents position in one half of the field to defend a goal. The third opponent, in the opposite goal area with a ball, starts play with a goal kick aimed toward the center circle. The team stationed in the center circle receives and controls the ball, and then attacks the goal defended by two opponents to create a 3 vs. 2 player situation. The player who took the goal kick sprints the length of the field to help his or her teammates defend the goal. The two defending players try to delay the attackers until their teammate arrives. All shots at goal must be taken from within the penalty area. Play continues until a goal is scored or the defenders gain the ball. Restart each round with a goal kick. Teams alternate playing as defenders and attackers.

Scoring: Team scoring the most goals wins.

Practice Tips: This game is excellent fitness training for older players because of the long recovery runs required of the server. It is not appropriate for young children because of the physical demands on the players.

78

Splitting the Defense (4 vs. 2)

Minutes: 30 **Players:** Unlimited (groups of 6)

Objectives: Develop passing combinations that penetrate (split) the defense; practice correct positioning of the first (pressuring) and second (covering) defenders

Setup: Using markers, outline a rectangular area 12 by 24 yards for each group. Station all 6 players within the area, 4 as attackers (with the ball) and 2 as defenders.

Procedure: Attackers keep the ball from the defenders by interpassing among themselves, and attempt to "split" (pass the ball between) defenders when the opportunity arises. (This is known as the "killer" pass.) If a defender steals the ball, or if the ball leaves the playing area, the ball is returned to an attacker. Continue for 10 minutes, then designate 2 different players as defenders. Play three rounds, all players taking a turn as defenders.

Scoring: Attacking team gets 1 point for 8 consecutive passes without loss of possession and 2 points for a completed pass that splits the defenders. Defenders get 1 point each time they gain possession of the ball. Attackers count their point total; defenders count theirs.

Practice Tips: Attackers should spread out and attack with width and depth. Players should adjust their support positioning as the ball changes location. Attackers should provide offensive support at wide angles to either side of the ball and should look to split the defense with killer passes. Defenders should pressure the attackers to limit their passing options. The defender farthest from the ball (also called the support or second defender) must cover any passing lanes to prevent the killer pass. For highly skilled players reduce the area and limit the number of touches allowed to pass and receive the ball.

79

Hot Potato (5 vs. 2)

Minutes: 15   **Players:** Unlimited (groups of 7)

Objectives: Maintain possession of the ball through combination passing; practice defending tactics used when outnumbered

Setup: Using markers, outline a rectangular area 15 by 20 yards for each group. Colored vests differentiate defenders from attackers. Each group has a ball.

Procedure: Attackers attempt to keep the ball from defenders by completing as many consecutive passes as possible. Attackers are limited to three or fewer touches to receive and pass the ball. If a defender steals the ball, the ball goes out of play, or an attacker uses more than three touches to control and play the ball, the attackers start over again. Defenders who steal the ball immediately return it to an attacker and the game continues.

Scoring: Attacking team gets 2 points for 10 consecutive passes. Defenders get 1 point each time they intercept a pass or force the attackers to lose control of the ball outside the playing area. Play until either defenders or attackers total 10 points. Repeat with 2 different players as defenders.

Practice Tips: The game is called "Hot Potato" because the ball constantly moves from one attacker to another. Adjust the area to the age and abilities of players. For a more challenging game reduce the area or add restrictions on the attacking players (for example, one- or two-touch passing only).

80

4 vs. 2 (Plus 2)

Minutes: 15-20   **Players:**   8 (two teams of 4)

Objectives: Develop group tactics in attack and practice defending when outnumbered

Setup: Using markers, outline a rectangular area 40 by 25 yards. Use cones or flags to represent two goals 5 yards wide and about 10 yards apart on each end line. One team has a ball.

Procedure: Each team defends two goals and can score in either of the opponent's goals. The team with possession attacks with 4 players; their opponents defend with 2 field players and a goalkeeper in each goal. If a defending player steals the ball he or she must first pass it back to one of his or her goalkeepers before the team can begin their counterattack. Otherwise regular soccer rules apply.

Scoring: Team scoring the most goals wins.

Practice Tips: Emphasize immediate transition from defense to attack and vice versa upon change of possession. Impose restrictions (for example, two-touch passing only) to make the game more challenging for advanced players.

81

Immediate Attack (5 vs. 3)

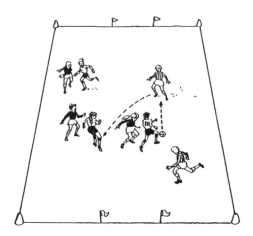

Minutes: 15-20   **Players:**   8

Objectives: Practice the group tactics used in attack and defense; organize a swift counterattack upon gaining possession of the ball; develop endurance

Setup: Using markers, outline a rectangular area 30 by 50 yards. Place a goal 4 yards wide at the center of each end line. Organize two teams of 3 players each, the 2 remaining players being neutrals. Colored scrimmage vests differentiate the teams and the neutrals. There are no goalkeepers. One team has the ball.

Procedure: Start the game with a kickoff from the center of the area. The neutrals play with the team in possession to create a 5 vs. 3 player advantage for the attack. Teams score by kicking the ball through the opponents' goal below waist height. When a defending player wins the ball his or her first pass must be to one of the neutrals in order to start the counterattack. Otherwise regular soccer rules apply.

Scoring: Team scoring the most goals wins.

Practice Tips: Emphasize immediate transition from defense to attack after gaining possession of the ball. For advanced players use regulation goals and goalkeepers. Reduce the area for younger players.

82

Double Zone Soccer (3 vs. 2)

Minutes: 20-25   **Players:**   12 (two teams of 6)

Objectives: Develop the defending and attacking tactics used in a 3 vs. 2 situation

Setup: Using markers, outline a rectangular area 35 by 50 yards, bisected by a midline. Place a regulation goal at each end of the field. Designate 3 players as attackers and 2 as defenders for each team. Station the attackers for each team in the opponents' half of the field and the defenders for each team in their own half. This creates a 3 vs. 2 situation in each zone. Position a goalkeeper in each goal. Colored scrimmage vests differentiate teams. One team has the ball.

Procedure: Each team defends its goal and attacks the opponents' goal. Attackers and defenders are restricted to movement within their assigned zone. Defenders who steal the ball pass to a teammate in the opponents' half of the field to start the counterattack. After a goal is scored the team scored against gains possession of the ball.

Scoring: Team scoring the most goals wins.

Practice Tips: Since defending players are outnumbered in their zone they cannot play 1-on-1 defense. One defender should pressure the opponent with the ball. The second defender positions to prevent a killer pass that would split the defenders and create an opportunity for the attack to score.

Defenders should reposition and change roles depending on the ball's movement. Attackers should use quick passing combinations and player movement off the ball to free the extra attacker for a strike on goal.

83

Score Through Back Door or Front Door

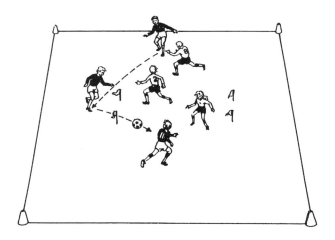

Minutes: 15-20   **Players:** Two equal teams of 3-5

Objectives: Develop passing combinations and player movement away from the ball; develop endurance

Setup: Using markers, outline a square 30 by 30 yards. Use cones or flags to represent two small goals within the area. There are no goalkeepers. One ball required.

Procedure: Begin with a kickoff from the center of the area. Regular soccer rules apply, except that teams can score by kicking the ball through either goal. In addition, shots may be taken from both sides of the goals, scoring through the "back door" or the "front door."

Scoring: Team scoring the most goals wins.

Practice Tips: Require teams to use 1-on-1 marking of opponents. Stress the importance of immediate transition between defense and attack on change of possession. As a variation add a third goal.

84

In and Out (Half Court Soccer)

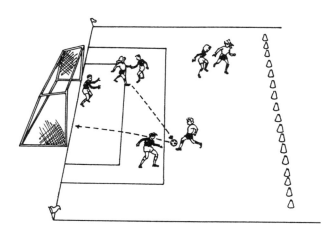

Minutes: 25-30   **Players:** Two teams of 3 plus 1 neutral

Objectives: Develop the group tactics used in attack and defense; improve fitness

Setup: Play on one half of a regulation field with a goal positioned on the end line. Place a line of markers spanning the width of the field 35 yards from goal. Station the attacking team outside the 35-yard zone, with the ball. Defenders station in the 35-yard zone. The neutral player is goalkeeper.

Procedure: The attacking team enters the defending zone and attempts to score. Change of possession occurs when the ball goes out of play, a foul or misconduct occurs, a goal is scored, the goalkeeper saves a shot, or a defender steals the ball. Teams alternate playing attack and defense depending upon who has possession of the ball. Each new attack must begin outside the 35-yard zone. Otherwise regular soccer rules apply.

Scoring: Team gets 2 points for each goal scored and 1 point for a shot on goal saved by the keeper. The team scoring the most points wins.

Practice Tips: Virtually all small group tactics can be practiced in a 3 vs. 3 situation. Emphasize the concepts of width, depth, and penetration in attack. On defense emphasize the roles of the first (pressure), second (cover), and third (balance) defenders.

85

Attacking When Outnumbered

Minutes: 20   **Players:** 7 (three teams of 2 and 1 neutral)

Objectives: Develop the tactics and teamplay used when attacking in a numbers down (fewer players) situation; improve shooting skills; develop endurance

Setup: Using markers, outline a rectangular area 30 by 40 yards with a regulation goal on one end line. Station three teams within the area. Colored scrimmage vests differentiate teams. The neutral player is goalkeeper.

Procedure: The goalkeeper begins play by tossing the ball toward a far corner of the playing area. Teams vie for possession. The team winning the ball attacks the goal and the other two teams defend. If a defending player steals the ball his or her team immediately attacks and tries to score. The neutral goalkeeper attempts to save all shots. After a goal is scored, or the ball goes out of play, or a save is made, the goalkeeper resumes play by punting or throwing the ball to a far corner of the area.

Scoring: Team gets 1 point for a shot on goal and 2 points for a goal scored. The team scoring the most points wins.

Practice Tips: The attacking team is always outnumbered down (2 vs. 4). Attackers can isolate defending players by using one- and two-touch passes combined with creative dribbling. The give-and-go (wall) pass is also an effective tactic to use for attacking when outnumbered.

86

Scoring Off of a Back Pass

Minutes: 25   **Players:**   7 (two teams of 3 and 1 neutral)

Objectives: Create scoring opportunities against a packed defense; improve shooting technique; develop passing combinations used in the attacking third of the field

Setup: Play on one half of a regulation field with a regulation goal positioned on the end line. Colored scrimmage vests differentiate teams. Both teams score in the common goal. The goalkeeper is neutral and tries to save all shots.

Procedure: The goalkeeper begins play by tossing the ball to a far corner of the area where teams vie for possession. Basic soccer rules apply, except that points may be scored only from shots taken off of a ball passed back out of the penalty area. After a goal is scored, or the goalkeeper makes a save, or after the ball goes over the end line, the goalkeeper restarts play by tossing the ball to a far corner of the area.

Scoring: Team gets 1 point for a shot on goal saved by the goalkeeper and 2 points for a goal scored. The team scoring the most points wins.

Practice Tips: A back pass from a crowded penalty area is one of the best ways to free an attacker for a shot on goal. Reduce the penalty area for players 12 years and under.

87

Triangular Goal Game

Minutes: 25   **Players:** Two equal teams of 3-5

Objectives: Practice attacking and defending in small groups; improve defensive marking and cover; develop endurance

Setup: Using markers, outline a rectangular area 40 by 60 yards. Position three cones or flags to form a triangle in each half of the field. Make each side of the triangles 4 yards long. There are no goalkeepers. Colored scrimmage vests differentiate teams. Give one team possession of the ball to start the game.

Procedure: Goals are scored by shooting the ball through any side of the opponents' triangular goal. Defending players are responsible for protecting all sides of their goal and should continually reposition in response to the ball's location. Regular soccer rules apply, except that the offside law is waived.

Scoring: Team gets 1 point for a shot that travels through a side of the goal below knee height. The team that scores the most points wins.

Practice Tips: Defending players should always try to position between the goal they are defending and the ball. This is commonly referred to as a "goal-side" position.

88

6 vs. 4

Minutes: 25-30   **Players:** 11

Objectives: Develop the team tactics used in attack and defense

Setup: Using markers, outline a rectangular area 50 by 60 yards. Place a regulation goal on one end line. With cones or flags, mark two small goals (3 yards wide) 20 yards apart on the opposite end line. Designate a team of 6 attackers who play against a team of 4 defenders and a goalkeeper. Colored scrimmage vests differentiate teams. Station the keeper in the regulation goal. There are no goalkeepers in the small goals. Give attackers the ball to start the game.

Procedure: Attackers try to score in the regulation goal. Defenders gain possession by intercepting passes, by tackling the ball from an attacker, or by receiving the ball from the goalkeeper after a save or after a goal has been scored. On gaining possession the defending team tries to score in either of the small goals. Play is continuous.

Scoring: Attacking team gets 2 points for a goal and 1 point for a shot on goal saved by the goalkeeper. Defending team gets 1 point each time they kick the ball through either of the small goals. The team that scores the most points wins.

Practice Tips: Because defending players are outnumbered, they cannot play strict 1-on-1 defense. Defenders should attempt to protect the most critical space, the central areas from which goals are most likely to be scored. To make the game more challenging for the attacking team add restrictions (for example, two- or three-touch passing only).

89

Score by Dribbling Only

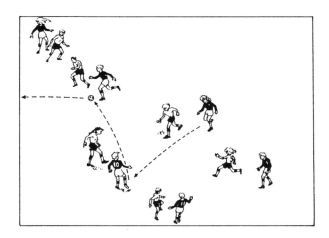

Minutes: 25   **Players:** 12-16 (two equal teams)

Objectives: Improve individual attacking and defending tactics in 1-on-1 situations; improve dribbling skills; develop endurance

Setup: Using markers, outline a rectangular area about 50 by 70 yards. Colored scrimmage vests differentiate teams. Give one team the ball.

Procedure: Begin with a kickoff from the center of the field. Each team defends an end line. Regular soccer rules apply, except that goals are scored by dribbling the ball over the opponents' end line rather than by shooting. The entire length of the end line is considered to be the goal line.

Scoring: Team gets 1 point each time a player dribbles the ball over the opponents' end line. The team scoring the most points wins.

Practice Tips: Require 1-on-1 defensive marking with each player assigned a specific opponent. Emphasize that players should take-on (dribble past) an opponent only in certain situations. In general, dribbling should be discouraged in a team's defending third of the field, where loss of possession may result in a goal against the team. Encourage players to take on opponents in the attacking third of the field nearest the opponents' goal. Beating a defender on the dribble in that area usually creates an opportunity to score a goal, and even if the dribbler loses possession it won't create an immediate danger to his or her own goal.

90

3-Team Game

Minutes: 25   **Players:** 14 (three teams of 4 plus 2 goalkeepers)

Objectives: Develop group tactics in attack and defense; develop endurance

Setup: Using markers, outline a rectangular area 70 by 40 yards with a regulation goal on each end line. Station one team to defend each goal and the third team with the ball at center field. Station a goalkeeper in each goal. Colored scrimmage vests differentiate teams.

Procedure: The team with the ball attacks and tries to score in one of the goals. If the ball is lost to the defending team, the goalkeeper makes a save, or a goal is scored, the original attacking team takes over defense of that goal while the original defending team moves forward to attack the opposite goal. Teams alternate playing on attack and defense. Regular soccer rules apply, except that the offside law is waived.

Scoring: Team gets 1 point for each goal scored. The team scoring the most points wins.

Practice Tips: Decrease the area and reduce the number of players per team to 3 for younger players. As an alternative, position two small goals on each end line and do not use goalkeepers.

91

No Contact Passing Game

Minutes: 25   **Players:**   Two teams of 5-8

Objectives: Develop passing combinations; improve the defensive skills and tactics used to intercept opponents' passes

Setup: Using markers, outline a rectangular area 50 by 70 yards with a field hockey goal at the center of each end line. Station teams in opposite halves of the field. There are no goalkeepers. Colored scrimmage vests differentiate teams. One team has the ball.

Procedure: Begin with a kickoff from the center of the field. Regular soccer rules apply, except that players are limited to three or fewer touches to receive, pass, and shoot the ball. Defending players gain possession only by intercepting passes. Tackling an opponent is prohibited. Teams switch from attack to defense and vice versa upon change of possession.

Scoring: Goals are scored by passing (not shooting) the ball through the opponents' goal. The team scoring the most goals wins.

Practice Tips: Defending players must anticipate opponents' passes and position to block passing lanes. Reduce the area for highly skilled players. Eliminate the "three touch" restriction for beginning players.

92

Game With Restricted Dribbling

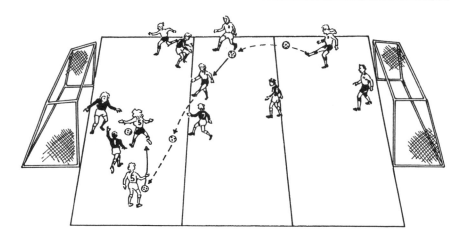

Minutes: 20   **Players:** 10 (two teams of 5)

Objectives: Practice the use of dribbling skills in appropriate situations and selected areas of the field; develop endurance

Setup: Using markers, outline a rectangular area 60 by 40 yards. Place a regulation goal on each end line. Use markers to divide the field lengthwise into three equal zones. Colored scrimmage vests differentiate teams. One player from each team positions as goalkeeper. One team has the ball.

Procedure: Start with a kickoff from the center of the field. Each team defends a goal and attempts to score in the other goal. Regular soccer rules apply, except for these restrictions. In the defending zone nearest their goal players may use only one- and two-touch passing. In the central zone players may dribble to advance the ball in open space but may not take-on and beat opponents. Dribbling is mandatory in the attacking third of the field, where players must beat an opponent by dribbling before passing to a teammate or shooting on goal. Violation of a zone restriction results in loss of possession to the opposing team.

Scoring: Team scoring the most goals wins.

Practice Tips: Dribbling skills are most effectively used to create scoring opportunities in the attacking third of the field where players can afford more risk because loss of possession there is not critical. Discourage excessive dribbling in the defending and central zones where loss of possession may produce a scoring opportunity for the opponents.

93

Soccer Keepaway

Minutes: 25

Players: 10 (two teams of four field players and a goalkeeper)

Objectives: Develop passing combinations used to maintain possession of the ball from opponents; develop group attacking and defending tactics; improve fitness

Setup: Using markers, outline a rectangular area 30 by 40 yards, with a goal 5 yards wide on each end line. Colored scrimmage vests differentiate teams. One team has the ball.

Procedure: Begin with a kickoff from the center of the field. Each team defends a goal. Teams score by kicking the ball through the opponent's goal below the height of the goalkeeper's shoulders, and/or by completing 10 consecutive passes. The defending team can gain possession of the ball by intercepting passes or tackling the ball from opponents. Except for the method of scoring, regular soccer rules apply.

Scoring: Team gets 1 point for a goal scored and 2 points for 10 consecutive passes. The team scoring the most points wins.

Practice Tips: Encourage players to have patience in organizing the attack, but alert them to look for and recognize the best time for a quick strike at goal. Teammates should strive to maintain possession until there is opportunity to move forward and score. Increase the area for less skilled players. For advanced players, require teams to use 1-on-1 marking to reduce the space and time available to the player with the ball.

94

3-Zone Game

Minutes: 25 **Players:** 12 (3 teams of 3; 1 neutral and 2 goalkeepers)

Objectives: Develop group tactics in attack and defense; improve endurance

Setup: Using markers, outline a rectangular area 40 by 60 yards. Place a regulation goal on each end line, using markers to divide the field into three equal zones 40 by 20 yards. Station a team in each zone and a goalkeeper in each goal. Colored scrimmage vests differentiate teams. The team in the middle zone has the ball. The neutral player always plays with the team in possession of the ball.

Procedure: The team in the middle zone, assisted by the neutral player, moves forward to score in one of the end zones. The defending team gains the ball when a pass is intercepted, when the goalkeeper makes a save, when a goal is scored, or when the ball travels over the end line. The original defending team then moves into the middle zone to become attackers, and the original attacking team remains in the end zone to play as defenders. The neutral player always joins the attacking team in the middle zone to create a 4 vs. 3 player advantage. A ball out of play over a sideline is returned by a throw-in.

Scoring: Team scoring the most goals wins.

Practice Tips: Players should make quick transitions from defense to attack after gaining possession. They should sprint from their defending zone into the middle zone, organize, and attack. Quick, precise passing combinations should be used to free an attacker for a strike on goal. In actual match situations any delay in the attack will allow defenders time to recover goalside of the ball to offset the numerical advantage.

95

4-Goal Game

Minutes: 25   **Players:** Two equal teams of 5-8

Objectives: Improve ability to change point of attack; develop endurance

Setup: Using markers, outline a square area 50 by 50 yards. Use cones or flags to represent a small goal 3 to 4 yards wide on the center of each of the 4 sidelines. Colored scrimmage vests differentiate teams. One team has the ball.

Procedure: Begin with a kickoff from the center of the field. Each team defends two goals and can score in two goals. Coach designates which goals each team defends and attacks. Teams score by shooting the ball through either of the opponents' goals below waist height. There are no goalkeepers. Regular soccer rules apply, except that the offside law is waived.

Scoring: Team scoring the most goals wins.

Practice Tips: Restrictions can be placed on advanced players to make the game more challenging (for example, limit of two touches to pass and receive the ball). As a variation, play with two balls at the same time.

96

Tight Marking Game

Minutes: 25   **Players:** Two equal teams of 5-8

Objectives: Improve 1-on-1 marking ability; develop endurance

Setup: Using markers, outline a rectangular area 50 by 75 yards with a goal 4 yards wide at the center of each end line. Colored scrimmage vests differentiate teams. There are no goalkeepers. One team has the ball.

Procedure: Begin with a kickoff from the center of the field. Each team defends a goal. Require strict 1-on-1 marking of all players. Because shots may be taken from anywhere on the field marking must be very tight to prevent long-range goals. Change of possession occurs when a defender steals the ball, when the ball goes out of play, or when a goal is scored.

Scoring: The team scoring the most goals wins.

Practice Tips: Reduce the area to further limit the time and space available for highly skilled players. As a variation place multiple small goals along the end lines to provide additional options for attackers.

97

Game With Wingers

Minutes: 25

Players: 10 (two teams of 3, two neutrals, two goalkeepers)

Objectives: Improve flank play; practice scoring off of balls crossed from the flanks

Setup: Using markers, outline a rectangular area 50 by 40 yards, with a regulation goal on each end line. Mark a zone 5 yards wide, extending the length of the field, on each flank. Organize two teams of 3 players each. Designate 2 additional players as wing forwards (wingers) who station in opposite flank zones. Station a goalkeeper in each goal. One team has the ball.

Procedure: Begin with a kickoff from the center of the field. Teams play 3 vs. 3 in the central zone. The wing players are neutral and play with the team that has the ball to create a 5 vs. 3 advantage. Goals can be scored directly from the central zone or from balls crossed into the goal area by the wing forwards. Wingers are restricted to movement within their flank zones. When a winger receives a pass from a central player or the goalkeeper, he or she must dribble to the opponents' end line and cross the ball into the goal area. Otherwise regular soccer rules apply.

Scoring: Team scoring the most goals wins.

Practice Tips: This game teaches players to spread apart opposing defenders by incorporating wing play into the attack. Passing the ball into a flank area causes defenders to readjust their position, which often creates gaps in the defense, possibly leading to scoring opportunities.

98

Pass, Dribble, or Shoot to Score

Minutes: 25   **Players:** Two equal teams of 6

Objectives: Develop the individual and group tactics used in attack and defense; improve endurance

Setup: Using markers, outline a rectangular area 50 by 70 yards, with a regulation goal on each end line. Place cones or flags to represent a small goal 2 yards wide on each flank of the area. Station teams in opposite halves of the field, each with a goalkeeper in the regulation goal. Colored vests differentiate teams. One team has the ball.

Procedure: Begin with a kickoff from the center of the field. Players score points by shooting the ball past the opposing goalkeeper into the large goal, passing the ball through either of the small goals to a teammate on the opposite side of the goal, and/or dribbling the ball over the opponents' end line. Players may score through the small goals in either direction. Except for the method of scoring, regular soccer rules apply.

Scoring: Team gets 3 points for a scoring in the regulation goal, 1 point for a pass completed to a teammate through a flank goal, and 1 point for a ball dribbled over the opponents' end line. The team scoring the most points wins.

Practice Tips: Since the attacking team has multiple scoring options, require tight 1-on-1 marking all over the area.

Restarts

99

Throw It Long

Minutes: 10   **Players:**   Unlimited (in pairs)

Objectives: Improve throw-in distance and accuracy

Setup: Partners face one another from opposite halves of a regulation field. To begin each player should station about 10 yards from the midline. Each pair has a ball.

Procedure: Partners toss the ball back and forth, trying to throw it as far as possible, using the correct throw-in motion. Players try to catch the ball out of the air and return it by throwing from the spot where they received it. The player who eventually forces his or her partner the farthest distance from the midline due to the cumulative distances of his or her throws wins. Players may advance beyond centerline.

Scoring: None

Practice Tips: The ball must be released from behind the head with both hands behind the ball. To generate maximum distance on the throw players should arch their upper body backwards from the waist and then snap forward as they release the ball. The player's feet must be in contact with the ground at the moment of release. Reduce the initial throwing distance for younger players.

100

Throw-In at Moving Targets

Minutes: 10-15   **Players:**   9 (three teams of 3)

Objectives: Improve throw-in accuracy; improve mobility and agility

Setup: Organize players into teams of three. Using markers, outline a rectangular area 45 by 20 yards, divided into three equal zones. Position a team in each zone. Players in the end zones are "throwers" and players in the middle zone are "targets." One thrower in each end zone has a ball.

Procedure: Throwers attempt to hit targets below the waist with a ball. The proper throw-in motion must be used. The targets are free to move about within their zones to avoid being contacted by a ball. Balls traveling through the central zone are collected by players in the opposite end zone who in turn throw to hit the targets. A central player hit with a thrown ball immediately returns it to any one of the throwers and play continues.

Scoring: Team gets 1 point for each target contacted below the waist with a ball. Assess 1 penalty point for each illegal throw as judged by the coach. The first team to score 15 points wins the round. Play three rounds.

Practice Tips: Throws must contact targets below the waist. Rotate teams after each round with players from an end zone moving into the middle zone.

101

Throw-In Game

Minutes: 15   **Players:**   Two equal teams of 4-6

Objectives: Improve throw-in technique

Setup: Using markers, outline a rectangular area 30 by 50 yards, with a goal 4 yards wide on the center of each end line. Station teams in opposite halves of the field. Colored scrimmage vests differentiate teams. There are no goalkeepers. One team has a ball.

Procedure: Passing among teammates is accomplished by throwing and catching, not kicking, the ball. Proper throw-in motion is required for all throws. Players may take a maximum of five steps with the ball before releasing it. Change of possession occurs when a throw is intercepted, the ball drops to the ground, a goal is scored, a player makes an improper throw-in, or the ball travels out of bounds. Balls out of bounds are returned by throw-in. Goals are scored by throwing the ball through the opponents' goal. Although goalkeepers are not designated, all players may use their hands to block shots aimed at their goal. The coach, or an extra player, officiates the game.

Scoring: Team scoring the most goals wins.

Practice Tips: Emphasize the correct throw-in technique. Both hands are placed behind the ball and the throwing motion must begin from behind the head. Both feet must be in contact with the ground at the moment the ball is released.

102

Direct Kick Competition

Minutes: 20   **Players:** 5 (two teams of 2 plus 1 goalkeeper)

Objectives: Develop the ability to score from direct free kicks

Setup: Using markers, outline a rectangular area 25 by 40 yards. Place a regulation goal on one end line and use markers to indicate a small goal 4 yards wide on the opposite end line. Use cones to divide the field lengthwise into two equal halves. Station the goalkeeper in the regulation goal. One team has the ball.

Procedure: The attacking team attempts to score from a direct free kick spotted on the midline 20 yards from the goal. Defending team players must stand to the side of the goal while the kick is taken. Attacking team gets one additional free kick each time the shooter scores. If the goalkeeper saves the shot, he or she gives the ball to one of the defending players. The defending team then moves forward and tries to score through the small goal while the original attacking team defends it. Play continues until either a goal is scored through the small goal or the ball leaves the area. After stopping play, restart the next round with a direct free kick from the midline. Teams and players alternate taking direct free kicks.

Scoring: Team gets 2 points for each goal scored in the regulation goal, and 1 point for each goal scored in the small goal. The team scoring the most points wins.

Practice Tips: Reduce the shooting distance for younger players. Encourage advanced players to develop the ability to swerve, or bend, the trajectory of their shots.

Part IV

GAMES FOR GOAL-
KEEPER TRAINING

The goalkeeper is often the forgotten player during training sessions. The majority of goalkeepers spend most of their practice time standing in goal with orders to stop all shots. Obviously that is not sufficient training for the player who is possibly the most important one on the team. The goalkeeper is a specialist and should be coached as such.

Goalkeepers must master a unique set of skills. These include the techniques used to receive low, medium, and high balls, skills used when diving to save, and the kicking and throwing skills used to distribute the ball back into play. The practice games described in this part are best suited to players who have previously been introduced to basic goalkeeping skills. The games can be used effectively to sharpen those skills as well as to supplement more intense goal-keeper training.

NOTE: Players under 12 years old should not specialize solely in the goalkeeper position. It is important that all players, even those who think they may want to be a goalkeeper, develop the basic foot skills used by field players. The changing role of the goalkeeper today requires that he or she be able to execute passing and receiving skills much more so than in the past.

103

Cushion and Catch

Minutes: 15   **Players:**   Unlimited (groups of 2)

Objectives: Improve ability to catch the ball; develop "soft" hands; develop mobility

Setup: Partners stand approximately 4 yards apart facing one another. Each player holds a ball in his or her left hand at approximately head height.

Procedure: Partners shuffle sideways across the width of the field while simultaneously tossing the ball from their left hand to their partner's right hand. Tosses must be received with one hand only. Repeat for 10 widths of the field.

Scoring: Assess 1 penalty point each time a player drops the ball and 1 penalty point for an inaccurate toss to a partner. Each keeper keeps total of his or her points. Player with the *least* number of penalty points wins.

Practice Tips: Encourage goalkeepers to maintain balance and body control at all times. They should never cross their legs as they shuffle sideways. Experienced keepers can make the game more challenging by increasing the velocity of their tosses.

104

Skippers

Minutes: 15   **Players:**   Unlimited (groups of 2)

Objectives: Develop ability to save low-skipping shots

Setup: Using markers, outline a rectangular area 15 by 20 yards for each pair. Use cones or flags to mark a regulation-size goal on each end line. Designate one partner as "A" and the other as "B," and station one on each goal line. Goalkeeper A has the ball.

Procedure: Goalkeeper A attempts to score by throwing or half volleying the ball through the goal, past goalkeeper B. The ball must bounce (skip) low off the ground directly in front of keeper B, who may advance off his or her goal line to narrow the shooting angle. If B fails to hold the ball goalkeeper A may follow up his or her shot and attempt to score off the rebound. Goalkeepers take turns attempting to score against each other.

Scoring: Goalkeeper who allows the least points wins.

Practice Tips: Proper technique is required to secure and hold a low-skipping shot. Keepers should not try to catch the ball in the palms of the hands. The goalkeeper should align with the oncoming ball and dive forward to smother the shot by clutching the ball against the chest. Elbows and arms should be cradled underneath the ball to prevent it bouncing free.

105

Pingers

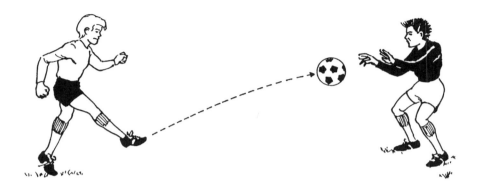

Minutes: 15   **Players:**   Unlimited (pairs)

Objectives: Develop ability to receive and hold powerful shots; develop "soft hands"

Setup: Partners face one another at a distance of approximately 10 yards. One has a ball.

Procedure: Partners take turns volleying (pinging) the ball back and forth from a distance of 8 to 10 yards. All volleys should be aimed at the partner's chest or head; diving to save is not required. The ball should be received on the fingertips and palms and not trapped against the body.

Scoring: Goalkeepers get 1 point for each shot they catch and hold in their hands. The keeper who totals the most points wins.

Practice Tips: Encourage goalkeepers to position their body behind the ball as a barrier. Head and hands are aligned with the oncoming ball with arms extended and slightly flexed at the elbow. Palms face forward with fingers spread and slightly extended.

106

Diving to Save

Minutes: 20   **Players:** Unlimited (pairs)

Objectives: Develop shot-saving ability

Setup: Using markers, outline a rectangular area 20 by 25 yards. Place a regulation goal on the center of each end line. If portable goals are not available, use cones or flags to represent goalposts. Station one goalkeeper in each goal. Designate one goalkeeper as "A" and one as "B." Give A possession of the ball.

Procedure: Goalkeeper A takes four steps in front of his or her goal line and attempts to volley or throw the ball past goalkeeper B. Keeper B may move forward to narrow the shooting angle before diving to save. After making a save B attempts to score against A from the spot where the save was made. Keepers alternate taking shots at one another until a goal is scored. After each score goalkeepers return to their respective goal lines to restart play.

Scoring: Players get points for preventing goals, not scoring them. Goalkeeper gets 2 points for a save caught and held, and 1 point for a save made by deflecting the ball wide (or over the regulation goal). The keeper who scores the most points wins.

Practice Tips: Encourage goalkeepers to move forward off their goal line to narrow the opponents' shooting angle. Keepers should try to catch and hold the ball when possible, rather than deflect it.

107

Hunting for Gold Nuggets

Minutes: 25 (five rounds of 5)

Players: 12-17 (including 2 goalkeepers)

Objective: Improve goalkeeper's ability to dispossess a dribbler in a break-away situation by smothering the ball

Setup: Station all players within the center circle of a field or an area of similar size. Each field player has a ball.

Procedure: Field players dribble to maintain possession within the circle. Goalkeepers attempt to steal "gold nuggets" by diving to the ground and smothering a ball. If a keeper steals a "nugget" he or she tosses it out of the circle and immediately goes after another. Goalkeepers try to capture as many gold nuggets as possible. Dribblers who lose their ball should quickly retrieve it and reenter the game.

Scoring: Goalkeeper gets 1 point for each ball captured. The keeper scoring the most points wins the round. Play five rounds.

Practice Tips: Adjust the area to the number of players. The area should not be too crowded with dribblers since that may increase the likelihood of player collisions. Encourage goalkeepers to smother the ball by diving and pinning it to the ground with their hands.

108

Saving the Breakaway

Minutes: 15   **Players:** Unlimited (groups of 2)

Objectives: Develop the goalkeeping skills used to save in a breakaway situation

Setup: Using markers, outline a rectangular area 20 by 25 yards for each group. Place cones or flags to represent a goal, 8 yards wide, on each end line. Each goalkeeper stations in a goal. Designate one goalkeeper "A" and the other "B." Goalkeeper A has the ball.

Procedure: Goalkeeper A dribbles forward from his or her goal area and tries to score against goalkeeper B by dribbling past or passing the ball underneath him or her. Long-range shooting is prohibited. Rebounds off the goalkeeper are playable. After a save or a goal, goalkeepers return to their respective goals. Keepers alternate turns attempting to score against each other.

Scoring: Since the primary focus of this game is goalkeeper training, points are given for saves, not goals. Goalkeepers get 1 point for each save of a breakaway situation. Goalkeeper who scores the most points wins.

Practice Tips: It is essential that goalkeepers learn the correct techniques used for saving breakaways before practicing those skills under simulated match conditions. As the dribbler approaches the keeper should move forward off the goal line. When nearing the dribbler the keeper should gradually lower into a crouch position with knees bent and arms extended down to sides. At the opportune moment he or she should go down to the side with arms extended toward the ball to make the save.

109

Breakaway Game

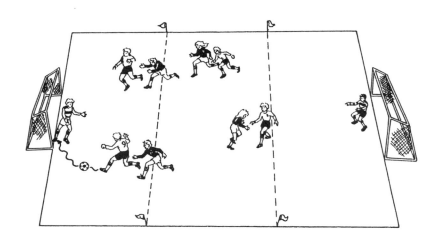

Minutes: 20   **Players:**   10 (two teams of 5)

Objectives: Improve goalkeepers' ability to save in a match-simulated breakaway situation

Setup: Using markers, outline a rectangular area 40 by 75 yards with a regulation goal on each end line. Use markers to divide the field lengthwise into 3 equal zones. Station both teams in the middle zone and a goalkeeper in each goal. Colored scrimmage vests differentiate teams. One team has the ball.

Procedure: Begin with a kickoff from the center of the field. The team with possession attempts to score via a breakaway, either by dribbling into its opponent's defending zone or penetrating by passing. Players from the defending team may not enter their defending zone before the ball does. This restriction forces the keeper to control the entire defending third and exposes him or her to a variety of breakaway situations. Regular soccer rules otherwise apply, except that the offside law is waived. Play is continuous.

Scoring: Goalkeeper gets 1 point for each save. The goalkeeper with the most points wins.

Practice Tips: Adjust the playing area to the age and abilities of players.

110

Cutting Off the Through Ball

Minutes: 15   **Players:** 7 (5 field players and 2 goalkeepers)

Objectives: Improve goalkeepers' ability to get to the ground quickly to smother passes, crosses, and through balls

Setup: Using markers, outline a rectangular area 15 by 25 yards for each group. Station field players around the perimeter of the area with two goalkeepers in the center. Field players have the ball.

Procedure: Field players pass to one another, trying to keep the ball from the goalkeepers. Limit field players to two or three touches to receive and pass the ball. All passes must be along the ground. Goalkeepers try to steal the ball by diving to the ground to intercept passes or smother the ball as a field player receives it. A goalkeeper who steals the ball immediately returns it to a field player and play continues.

Scoring: Goalkeepers get 1 point each time they steal the ball. Keeper scoring the most points wins.

Practice Tips: Adjust the area to the ability of the field players as well as that of the goalkeepers. Use a slightly larger area for advanced, highly experienced goalkeepers.

111

Shelling the Keeper

Minutes: (minimum) 7.5-10 (five rounds of 1.5-2)

Players: Unlimited (groups of 3)

Objectives: Improve goalkeeper's shot-saving ability

Setup: Play on one end of a regulation field with a regulation goal on the end line. Place 12 to 16 balls an equal distance apart on the front edge of the penalty area. Station 2 players as shooters 25 yards from the goal and the third player as goalkeeper.

Procedure: Shooters take turns running forward to shoot a stationary ball at goal. As soon as one player shoots and the keeper saves, the other shooter begins his or her approach to a ball. The keeper should have just enough time after each save attempt to position for the next shot. Continue the exercise until the supply of balls is used up.

Scoring: Goalkeeper gets 1 point for each save. Shooters get 2 points for each goal. The player (goalkeeper or shooter) scoring the most points wins the round. The first player to win 5 rounds wins the game.

Practice Tips: As always, require goalkeepers to wear appropiate clothing (padded shorts, long-sleeved shirts with padded elbows) to reduce the chance of injury. Reduce the shooting distance for younger players.

112

Angle Action

Minutes: 15   **Players:** 9-11

Objectives: Improve the goalkeeper's positioning and shot-saving ability

Setup: Play on one end of a regulation field with a regulation goal on the end line. Station 8 to 10 players as shooters at various locations within the penalty area and a goalkeeper in goal. Each shooter has a ball.

Procedure: Each shooter in turn pushes the ball one or two steps to the side and shoots to score. The keeper quickly adjusts position to narrow the shooting angle, sets in the ready position, and attempts to save. Continue until all shooters have taken a shot, rest for a minute, and then repeat the round.

Scoring: Goalkeeper gets 1 point for each save and shooters get 1 point for each goal. The player(s) (goalkeeper or shooters) scoring the most points wins.

Practice Tips: Require all shots be taken from a distance of 15 yards or more.

113

Penalty Kick Competition

Minutes: 20   **Players:** 8 (two teams of 4)

Objectives: Improve goalkeepers' ability to save penalty kicks; develop field players' ability to score from penalty kicks

Setup: Play on one end of a regulation field with a regulation goal on the end line. Place a cone or flag 1 yard inside each goalpost on the goal line. Mark the penalty kick spot 12 yards front and center of the goal.

Procedure: Shooters alternate taking penalty kicks against the opposing goalkeeper. In accordance with Fédération Internationale de Football Association (FIFA) rules, goalkeepers must position with their feet touching the goal line and cannot move off the line until the ball has been kicked. Each shooter attempts 10 penalty kicks.

Scoring: Shooter gets 2 points for a shot that beats the goalkeeper in a corner of the goal between a goalpost and a flag, and 1 point for a shot that beats the keeper in the central area of the goal. The goalkeeper allowing the fewest points wins.

Practice Tips: Encourage goalkeepers to look for subtle hints, such as the angle of the kicker's approach or the position of his or her kicking foot, that may reveal the shooter's intentions.

114

Boxing Game

Minutes: 25   **Players:** 4-6 (two teams of 2-3 goalkeepers)

Objectives: Improve goalkeepers' ability to box high balls

Setup: Play on a volleyball court. Stretch a net or rope 6 to 8 feet high across the center of the court. Station one team on each side of the net. Flip a coin to decide which team serves first. Position the server behind his or her end line.

Procedure: The server punts the ball over the net so it lands within the opponents' court (to constitute a good serve). The receiving team plays the ball directly out of the air by boxing it. Keepers may use the one- or two-fisted boxing technique. Teammates are permitted to box the ball to one another before returning it over the net. A fault occurs when the serve or return fails to clear the net, the serve or return lands out-of-bounds, or the ball is allowed to drop to the ground. Only the serving team can score points. A fault committed by the serving team results in loss of serve.

Scoring: Serving team gets 1 point for each fault committed by the receiving team. The first team to score 21 points wins. Play three rounds.

Practice Tips: In matches the boxing technique is used to clear high balls that have been lofted into the goal area. Encourage goalkeepers to box the ball with a short, powerful extension of the arms. Hand(s) should be positioned side by side with both firmly making a fist. The ball should be contacted directly at its center.

115

Moving Targets

Minutes: 10   **Players:** Unlimited "targets" (2-4 goalkeepers)

Objectives: Improve goalkeepers' throwing accuracy; develop field players' endurance

Setup: Using markers, outline a rectangular area about 40 by 50 yards. Station all players within the area. All except goalkeepers are "targets." Each goalkeeper has a ball.

Procedure: Goalkeepers throw, attempting to hit the targets with the ball on an ankle or a foot. Targets are free to move anywhere within the area. Goalkeepers are permitted to run after the targets but must set and throw from a stationary position. Keepers should quickly retrieve errant tosses that leave the area.

Scoring: Goalkeeper gets 1 point for each target hit correctly with a thrown ball. Keeper scoring the most points wins.

Practice Tips: Require goalkeepers to use the baseball or javelin throw technique. This game is not appropriate for younger players who have not yet developed adequate throwing skills.

116

Target Throwing

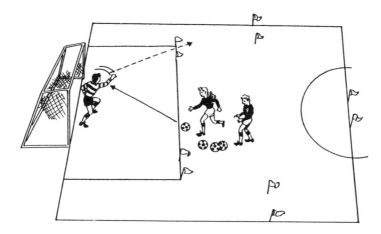

Minutes: 15   **Players:** Groups of 2-4 goalkeepers

Objectives: Improve goalkeepers' throwing accuracy

Setup: Each group plays on half of a regulation field. Use cones or flags to represent five small goals, each 3 to 4 yards wide. Position one goal within the center circle of the field, one on each flank about 35 yards from the end line, and one at each front corner of the penalty area. Station one goalkeeper in the regulation goal, with the others (servers) positioned 20 yards from goal with a supply of balls.

Procedure: Servers alternate taking shots at goal. The goalkeeper attempts to save each shot and then distributes the ball by attempting to throw it through a small goal. Require three attempts at each goal for a total of 15 throws. Repeat the round with a different goalkeeper in goal.

Scoring: Goalkeeper gets 1 point for a throw through either of the goals positioned at the edge of the penalty area, 2 points for a throw through the goals positioned on the flanks, and 3 points for a throw through the goal in the center circle.

Practice Tips: Goalkeepers can choose from several different throwing techniques. The rolling (bowling) or sidearm technique can be used over short distances, whereas the baseball- or javelin-type throw should be used to toss the ball over medium and long distances. This game is not appropriate for young players who do not possess the physical strength and ability to throw the ball far enough.

117

Target Kicking

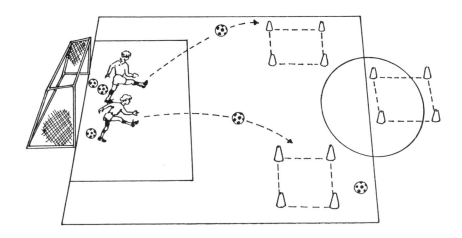

Minutes: 20   **Players:**   Unlimited (in pairs)

Objectives: Develop the ability to accurately distribute the ball by punting and drop-kicking

Setup: Play on three-quarters of a regulation field or area of similar size. Place cones or flags to designate three grids 10 by 10 yards at distances of between 40 and 60 yards from goal. Station goalkeepers within the penalty area with a supply of balls.

Procedure: Keepers alternate turns attempting to punt or drop-kick a ball into the grids. All kicks must be taken from within the penalty area. After all the balls have been kicked the keepers retrieve them, return to the penalty area, and repeat the drill. Keepers attempt 12 kicks into each grid for a total of 36 punts and/or dropkicks each.

Scoring: Goalkeeper gets 2 points for a ball that enters a grid on the fly and 1 point for a ball that rolls or bounces into or through a grid. The goalkeeper scoring the most points wins.

Practice Tips: Vary the size of the grids and their distance from goal, depending upon the age and abilities of players. For older, more experienced goalkeepers make the grids smaller. Reduce the number of punts and/or dropkicks for younger players.

118

Defending the Central Goal

Minutes: 25   **Players:**   7 (two teams of 3 plus 1 neutral goalkeeper)

Objectives: Develop the goalkeepers' shot-saving ability; improve mobility and footwork

Setup: Using markers, outline a rectangular area 30 by 40 yards. Place cones or flags in the center of the area to represent a regulation goal. The goalkeeper has the ball.

Procedure: The goalkeeper tosses the ball to a far corner of the area, where teams vie for possession. Regular soccer rules apply except that goals may be scored through the central goal from either side. The goalkeeper moves from one side of the goal to the other in response to the changing location of the ball. After each save or goal scored the keeper restarts play.

Scoring: A shot traveling between the goalposts below the height of the goalkeeper's head counts as a goal scored. Attacking team gets 1 point for each goal. Keeper gets 1 point for each save. Players keep tally of their points. Goalkeeper or team with most points wins.

Practice Tips: Place restrictions on field players to emphasize a specific aspect of goalkeeper training. For example, require that all goals be scored in breakaway situations. As a safety precaution for younger players, designate neutral zones in front of each goal that attacking players may not enter. This will prevent collisions between field players and the goalkeeper.

119

4 vs. 4 vs. 2 Keepers

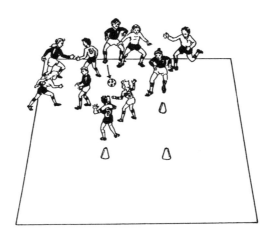

Minutes: 25   **Players:**   10 (8 field players and 2 goalkeepers)

Objectives: Develop goalkeepers' shot-saving ability; improve goalkeepers' mobility and footwork

Setup: Organize two teams of 4 field players and one goalkeeper each. Using markers, outline a square area about 40 by 40 yards. Place cones or flags to represent the corners of a square 8 by 8 yards in the center of the area. Each side of this square represents a goal. Prior to the start of the game designate which goals each team defends and attacks. One team has the ball.

Procedure: Begin with a throw-in from outside the area. Each team can score through two sides of the square goal and must defend two sides. Since each goalkeeper defends two goals he or she must shift from one to the other depending upon the movement of the ball. Regular soccer rules apply except that the offside law is waived.

Scoring: The goalkeeper allowing the fewest goals wins.

Practice Tips: Require keepers to use the sideshuffle foot movement when moving sideways to position for a save, and when moving from one goal to another. Keepers should never cross their legs when shuffling sideways.

120

Scoring From High Balls

Minutes: 25   **Players:**   14 (two equal teams of 7)

Objectives: Develop goalkeepers' ability to receive and control high balls:
develop field players' ability to serve long accurate passes; develop endurance

Setup: Using markers, outline a rectangular area 70 by 50 yards. Use
cones or flags to mark a "goalbox" 10 by 10 yards at each end of the area.
Position a goalkeeper in each box. Colored scrimmage vests differentiate
teams. One team has the ball.

Procedure: Begin with a kickoff from the center of the field. Teams defend
the goalbox on their end of the field and score by serving a lofted pass into
the opponent's goalbox so that the opposing goalkeeper can catch the ball
directly out of the air. Goalkeepers are not permitted to leave the goalbox
to receive the ball. After a goalkeeper catches the ball he or she sends it to
a teammate and play continues. Other than the method of scoring regular
soccer rules apply.

Scoring: Team gets 1 point for each lofted pass that the opposing goalkeeper receives directly out of the air. Team scoring the most points wins.

Practice Tips: Encourage goalkeepers to extend the arms up and receive
the ball at the highest possible point. Allow field players to serve (shoot) the
ball from anywhere on the field. This will require defending players to use
tight marking of opponents to prevent long-range scores.

Soccer Terms Defined

attacker(s)—The player(s) in possession of the ball.

back pass—Attacker passes the ball backwards, toward his or her own goal, to a supporting teammate.

balance—Positioning of defending players away from the ball to provide depth and support.

ball juggling—Keeping the ball airborne by using various body surfaces.

baseball throw—Technique used to toss the ball over medium distances. Ball is held in palm of throwing hand and released with a motion resembling a baseball toss.

block tackle—Defender uses the inside surface of the foot to block, or tackle, the ball from an opponent.

body feints—Misleading movements a player dribbling the ball uses to unbalance or outmaneuver an opponent.

boxing—Technique used to clear high balls out of the goal area; also called *punching*. The goalkeeper forms two solid fists with hands held together to strike the ball.

breakaway—Situation where an attacker with the ball breaks free of defenders and creates a one-on-one situation with the goalkeeper.

chip pass—A pass that is lofted over an opponent.

combination pass—Passing among teammates.

commit the defender—Attacker dribbles at and draws a defending player into a poor defensive position.

cover—Defensive support. As the defender nearest the ball challenges for possession he or she is supported from behind (covered) by a teammate.

crab position—Sitting position with buttocks elevated off the ground by the arms and legs.

defender(s)—Player(s) on the team that does not have the ball.

direct free kick—A free kick that can score a goal directly (the ball does not have to touch another player).

dive header—To dive parallel to the ground to head a low driven ball. Contact is made with the forehead.

endurance training—Preparation to function at maximal efficiency for an entire match.

far post—The goalpost farther from the ball.

first defender—Defender nearest the ball.

first-time shooting—Shooting the ball with the first touch, without first controlling it.

forward(s)—Front-running players; also called *strikers*.

free kick—Kick awarded to a team for a foul committed by opponents.

goal-side position—Defending player's position between his or her goal and the opponent to be marked (see **one-on-one marking**).

half-volley shot—Striking a ball dropping from above with the instep surface of the foot at the instant it contacts the ground.

heading technique—Ball should be contacted on the forehead with eyes open and mouth closed.

indirect free kick—A free kick that cannot score a goal directly (the ball must be touched by another player before entering the goal).

inside-of-foot pass—A pass using the inside surface of the foot; used for short-range passes.

instep drive—A stationary or rolling ball is contacted with the instep surface of the foot.

instep pass—A pass using the foot's full instep surface; used for medium- and long-range passes.

interpassing—Combination passing among teammates.

javelin throw—Technique used to toss the ball over long distances. Throwing arm is fully extended behind body with ball held between hand and wrist. Throwing motion is whiplike in an upward arc.

jump header—To jump upward and head the ball off the forehead.

mobility—Ability to move about quickly and fluidly.

near post—The goalpost nearer the ball.

nutmeg—Dribbling maneuver that pushes the ball between the legs of a defender.

one-on-one marking—Defensive tactic whereby each defender is responsible for guarding a specific opponent.

one-touch passing—Passing without stopping the ball; also called first-time passing.

outside-of-foot pass—A pass using the outside surface of the instep; used for short- and medium-range passes.

penalty kick—A direct free kick awarded to the attacking team when a defending player commits a direct foul within his or her own penalty area. The kick is taken from the penalty spot 12 yards front and center of the goal.

poke tackle—Defender reaches in with leg extended and uses the toes to poke the ball away from an opponent.

punching—See **boxing**.

receiving surface—The body surface used to receive and control the ball; commonly the inside or outside surface of the foot, the thigh, or the chest.

rolling—Also called *bowling*. Method of distributing the ball over short distances. Goalkeeper cups ball in palm of hand, steps toward intended target, bands forward from the waist, and releases the ball with a bowling-type motion.

second defender—Defender who takes up a position to protect (cover) the space directly behind the first defender (defender nearest the ball).

shielding—Attacker positions his or her body between the opponent and the ball to maintain possession.

sidearm throw—Used to distribute the ball over short and medium distances. Goalkeeper holds ball in palm at shoulder height, steps toward target, and releases the ball at about waist height as arm swings forward on a slightly downward plane.

side-shuffle—Moving sideways without crossing the feet; footwork used by the goalkeeper.

slide tackle—Defender slides on side to kick the ball away from an opponent.

smother—To dive and pin the ball to the ground with the hands.

striker(s)—Front-running player(s); also called *forward(s)*.

support—Movement of attacking players into positions that provide passing options for a teammate with the ball; movement of defending players into positions to cover a teammate attempting to gain possession of the ball.

tackle—To dispossess an opponent of the ball.

tactics—Individual tactics are planned maneuvers of a player in a one-on-one situation. Group tactics are planned, coordinated maneuvers of a cooperating group of players. Team tactics are planned, coordinated maneuvers of the entire team.

take-on—To dribble at and attempt to beat an opponent.

takeover—To exchange possession of the ball with a teammate while dribbling. As teammates approach one another from opposite directions, the player with the ball leaves it for his or her teammate.

third defender(s)—Defender(s) who protect the space behind the second (covering) defender on the side of the field opposite the ball.

throw-in—Prescribed method of returning a ball into play that has traveled out of bounds over a sideline (touchline) of the field. The ball must be held with two hands and released directly over the head. Both feet must be touching the ground when the ball is released.

transition play—Immediate shift from attack to defense, or vice versa, upon change of possession.

two-touch passing—Controlling the ball with the first touch and passing with the second.

volley punt—Method of kicking the ball. Ball is held in palm of hand with arm extended in front of body. The ball is volleyed out of the hand using a snapping motion of the kicking leg.

volley shot—Striking the ball in the air with the instep surface of the foot.

wall pass—A combination pass with one player serving as a barrier to redirect the path of the ball. The player in possession passes to a teammate (the "wall") and immediately sprints forward into open space to receive a return pass. The wall pass is commonly referred to as the "give-and-go" pass.

warm-up—Exercises that prepare a player, both physically and mentally, for strenuous training or match play.

wingers—Forwards positioned on the flank areas.

zonal marking—Defensive system in which each player is responsible for defending a certain area of the field.

About the Author

Joe Luxbacher is a former professional player in the North American Soccer League, the American Soccer League, and the Major Indoor Soccer League. He is head soccer coach at the University of Pittsburgh and holds an "A" Coaching License from the United States Soccer Federation. Joe is director of Keystone Soccer Kamps and Shoot to Score Soccer Camps, and fitness editor for *Total Health* magazine.

Joe, who holds a PhD in the management and administration of physical education and athletics, has written seven other books, including *The Soccer Goalkeeper, Soccer: Steps to Success*, and *Teaching Soccer: Steps to Success*, all published by Human Kinetics. He also publishes articles on health and fitness, nutrition and athletic performance, outdoor recreation, sport psychology, and sport sociology. In his leisure, Joe enjoys hiking, horseback riding, and cross-country skiing.

DATE DUE

u'll find
tanding
urces at

www.   com

457

277 1555
465-7301
278 1708
309-1890

Demco

HUMAN KINETICS
The Premier Publisher for Sports and Fitness
P.O. Box 5076 • Champaign, IL 61825-5076 USA